NAPOLEON AND THE JEWS

FRANZ KOBLER

NAPOLEON
AND THE JEWS

SCHOCKEN BOOKS · NEW YORK

the United States of America and Canada by
hocken Books Inc., New York 1976

Executive Editor: Henry Wasserman

Kobler, Franz, 1882—1965.
  Napoleon and the Jews.

  Bibliography: p.
  Includes index.
  1. Jews-Emancipation. 2. Jews — Restoration. 3. Assemblée des
Israélites de France et du royaume d'Italie, Paris, 1806—1807.
4. Paris. Sanhédrin, 1807. 5. Jews in France — History. 6. Napoléon I, Emperor of the French, 1769—1821. I. Title.
DS147.K57 1975   956.94'001   75-24509

© 1975 Leo Baeck Institute, New York and
Massada Press Ltd., Jerusalem

PRINTED IN ISRAEL
by Peli Printing Works Ltd.

CONTENTS

AFTERMATH OF THE NAPOLEONIC ERA

INTRODUCTION

The present study is intended to make a contribution both to the history of the Jewish people and to the biography of Napoleon Bonaparte. Various reasons prompted the rewriting of this particular chapter of Jewish and Napoleonic history.

Among the host of Napoleon's biographers none has so far paid much attention to the role which the Jewish people and the Jewish problem have played in Napoleon's life and political activities. Apart from mostly short references to the convocation of the Great Sanhedrin in Paris, only casual remarks about Napoleon's policy concerning the Jews can be discovered in the vast Napoleonic literature. Research and presentation of the subject have been left almost entirely to the writers on Jewish history. There are, in addition to chapters in general histories of the Jews, a considerable number of monographs and articles on the theme, "Napoleon and the Jews," written by Jewish scholars. But even here, it is mainly the legislation of the Emperor Napoleon that has been dealt with, while the pertinent events in Napoleon Bonaparte's early career have been neglected for a long time. Only with the rise of Zionism has interest in these happenings become intensified. The efforts of scholars, especially

7

as far as the main event of that period — the Proclamation to the Jews issued by Bonaparte during his invasion of Palestine in 1799 — was concerned, were seriously hampered by the scarcity of the then available sources.

It was, in fact, not until 1940 that the texts of the Proclamation and, incidentally, of an unknown covering letter were unearthed and published by me in *The New Judaea* 1 (London). In an accompanying series of articles, I made the first attempt to present a comprehensive narrative based on this find of Bonaparte's unique attempt to restore the Jewish people to its ancient homeland.[1] Subsequently various comments on the published texts and valuable additional research have been made by several authors, particularly, in a comprehensive Hebrew study by the historian N. M. Gelber.[2] Thus new light was thrown on the origin of the discovered document and on the events themselves. At the same time, the Proclamation* in its newly established wording assumed meaningful significance through the historic upheaval that led to the reemergence of the State of Israel.

For all these reasons, a thoroughly revised and substantially enlarged edition of the Proclamation, including the covering letter, and of the original historical account has become indispensable. One of the primary purposes of the present study is to tell the full story of Bonaparte's attempt to restore Israel, summing up all the available sources and the carefully examined results of recent research. Integral to the narrative is an account of the reaction Bonaparte's move en-

---

* In the present book this word with a capital initial P always indicates the above-mentioned Proclamation of 1799.

countered in the Jewish and gentile worlds, showing the ambiguity of the contemporary attitude which oscillated between a predominant indifference or hostility and an enthusiastic, though only sporadic, acceptance. This task involved the obligation to deal with the last Messianic movement — the Frankists — and, especially, with its Bohemian followers. It was this isolated group which, strangely enough, became instrumental in the eventual disclosure of the texts of the Proclamation and of the rabbinical covering letter. The persecution suffered by the sect gave occasion to the translation of the texts into the German language. This study contains the text and thorough analysis of this hitherto unpublished original document, containing the translation, along with a minute account of its origin and discovery.

The story of the Frankists of Prague, the only Jewish group to welcome the Proclamation, has to be told in full in order to reveal the mysterious link between the last Messianic movement and the first political attempt to restore Israel, as well as to provide the background for the account of the events which led to the preservation and discovery of the only extant documentary testimony to the issue of the Proclamation. A striking counterpart is offered by the commotion which Bonaparte's invasion of Palestine caused among the British advocates of the Restoration of the Jews. The impulse given to the Restoration movement by the events of 1798 and 1799 made itself felt throughout the next two decades and even later on. It was increased by the impression of the Great Sanhedrin of Paris, one of the most widely discussed events of the epoch. Napoleon's eventual downfall strengthened rather than diminished his impact on Jewish though and destiny. In fact,

the political reaction which followed made the Jews realize
the merits of Napoleon's rule. Even denunciation of Napoleon's "infamous decree" failed to suppress the memory of
the General and Emperor who had torn down the ghetto
walls.

At the same time, Bonaparte's call to rebuild Jerusalem and
to convene the Sanhedrin continued to reverberate throughout
the Jewish world. The growing legend of a Napoleon who set
the pattern for the revival of the Jewish State became a
driving force in Jewish history. Theodor Herzl, in a great
moment of his struggle for the realization of the Zionist
idea, referred to Napoleon as his precursor. In the public
debate that preceded the issue of the Balfour Declaration,
Israel Zangwill urged his countrymen to follow Napoleon's
example. Napoleon appeared in Nahum Sokolow's *History
of Zionism* at a time when the Palestine Mandate was being
discussed at the Peace Conference in Paris, as the main witness to the feasibility of reviving the political existence of
the Jewish nation. The unearthed text of the Proclamation,
included in *Three Historical Memoranda* of the Vaad Leumi
(the National Council of the Jews of Palestine) in 1947, was
able to testify to Israel's proper claims to the Holy Land before the General Assembly of the United Nations.

PART ONE

FIRST CONTACTS WITH THE JEWISH WORLD

1

BONAPARTE'S EARLY JEWISH STUDIES AND EXPERIENCES

"The island of Corsica never seems at any time in history to have given hospitality to a Jewish community." This surprising statement of Cecil Roth[3] about Bonaparte's native isle is the first of many strange contradictions in the history of Napoleon Bonaparte's relations with the Jews. The very absence of Jews in his neighborhood spurred his curiosity. The means of satisfying it was the same he used to still his insatiable thirst for knowledge: books, books, books. A large heap of notes drawn from the books he read in his youth has been preserved. One passion above all soon became predominant: the study of history. This, rather than a religious interest, made the Bible the subject of Napoleon's Jewish studies. A handwritten notice dated Ajaccio, 20 April, 1790,[4] emphasizes the historical character and the continuity of the books, records their exact dates according to Hebrew chronology, and stresses Moses' authorship of the five books of the Torah. This strictly historical presentation does not prevent him from considering the Scriptures as "the word of God" and describing Israel as the "people of God." No similar survey of the New Testament has been found. Bonaparte

13

also used to mirror himself in the light of biblical history. On St. Helena he retold the story of the scene when his uncle Lucien (the archdeacon who after the death of Bonaparte's father had become the head of the family) lay on his deathbed surrounded by all his relatives and addressed himself to Napoleon's elder brother Joseph, saying: "You are the oldest of the family, but there is the head of it (pointing to Napoleon), never lose sight of him."[5] To this episode Napoleon made the amazing remark: "This was a true disinheritance; it was the scene of Jacob and Esau." These words seem to provide surprising support to Sigmund Freud's theory that Napoleon identified himself with his elder brother, Joseph.[6]

The attempts of the young Napoleon, a son of Corsica, the island without Jews, to penetrate into the Jewish sphere were not confined to readings of the Scriptures. Thus, one is astonished to find among the various notes jotted down by the future leader of the Oriental Expedition one about the commerce of the kings of Israel, David and Solomon, maintained via the ports of the Red Sea, that of Elath being expressly mentioned.[7] At about the same time, Napoleon's attention was attracted by a special chapter in an English work dealing with the Portuguese Jews.[8] The rather extensive extract opens with the statement that the Portuguese Jews form a national body: They avoid mixing with the rest of the Jewish people, claiming a noble origin from the first families of the Babylonian captives. Napoleon also noted the important role "in commerce and arts" they played in Spain under Moors and the Christian kings and the privileges they enjoyed in France where they found refuge as victims of the Inquisition.

The *Géographie Moderne* by abbé de Lacroix furnished Bonaparte with general information about Judaism. He noted that Judaism is one of the principal religions of the world, having two branches: the Jewish and the Samaritan. He also copied: "Il y a beaucoup de juifs en Asie, en Afrique, peu en Europe. Pour les Samaritains, viz la branche, elle subsiste encore en Naplouse."[9] In the light of that what was to happen less than ten years later, when Bonaparte, treading the soil of Egypt and Palestine, went up to Nablus and beyond it, the quotation seems to assume the character of a clairvoyant presentiment which is only matched by that famous and almost unbelievable excerpt, "St. Hélène, petite île..." with which the principal manuscript of the notes breaks off. When Bonaparte read the first volume of Voltaire's "Essai sur l'histoire Générale et sur les Mœurs et l'Esprit des Nations depuis Charlemagne jusqu'à nos jours," in May, 1791, one particular item attracted his attention: "Il y avait 8000 juifs dans Rome lors du règne de Tibère qui en envoya 4000 en Sardaigne."[10] As the passage reads, it does not necessarily suggest that it refers to the story of the first persecution of the Jews in imperial Rome. Bonaparte was apparently mainly interested in the fact that Sardinia had, through the act of the Roman Emperor, acquired a Jewish settlement, in contrast to neighboring Corsica. It would be only logical if another comparison would have been evoked by that historical fact. As an admirer of General Pasquale de Paoli, the Corsican patriot who had freed Corsica from Genoese rule, Bonaparte was presumably informed about the attempt the "father of the Fatherland" had made during the short period of Corsica's independence to induce the Jewish community of Leghorn to send Jewish settlers to Corsica.

In the military school at Brienne, Bonaparte used to separate himself from the company of his colleagues, sit down under a tree, and read Torquato Tasso's *Liberated Jerusalem*. The roots of the powerful appeal which *Liberated Jerusalem* had for Bonaparte must be sought in his strong attachment to Corsica, whose history was an almost uninterrupted struggle for liberation. Only in 1755, under the leadership of Paoli, did the Corsicans win a decisive victory and obtain their independence. Soon France took possession of the island and Paoli himself became the governor. Nevertheless, many Corsicans were opposed to French rule. The Bonapartes — one of the noblest families of the island — stood at the forefront of this faction. As a boy, Napoleon had begun to write a poem about the liberty of Corsica which he recited with a drawn sword in his hand. In the military school at Brienne he did not cease denouncing the injustice, the ungenerosity of a war waged by a great people against a tiny nation. It is in the light of the state of mind which characterizes these early years that his love of Tasso's poem has to be understood. He identified Corsica with Jerusalem and found in the very title the expression of his boldest dreams, of his yearning for liberty, and of the drive to the Orient.

2

THE LIBERATOR OF THE GHETTO

Among the countless strategic achievements of Napoleon none has surpassed the military feats performed by the youthful Bonaparte in Italy. While the glories of Lodi, Montenotte, and Rivoli are undisputed, the deeds of Bonaparte, the rising statesman, have become a matter of controversy. In spite of the severity and harshness of some measures, his expansionist aims were coupled with a genuine liberating tendency. The Inquisition, feudal rights, all exclusive privileges were abolished, the number of monasteries was reduced, custom barriers between provinces were thrown down...Viewed in this light, it was he, and he alone, who carried through the Revolution. "Peoples of Italy, the French army comes to break your chains," reads the conclusion of a proclamation which Bonaparte issued on April 26, 1796. "The French people is the friend of all peoples, meet it with confidence. Your property, your religion, and your usages will be respected. We make war as generous enemies, and we have no quarrel save with tyrants who enslave you."[11]

The elements of freedom and national revival which were inherent in Bonaparte's victories and reflected in his procla-

17

mations became manifest in the treatment of the Jews. Deprived of the rights of citizens, humiliated in many places by the obligation of wearing the medieval yellow badge, confined to the secluded ghettos, the Jews of Italy offered Bonaparte the stirring sight of a persecuted minority. In every Italian city which the French army entered, the ghetto gates were removed, hacked to pieces and burned, the shameful badges thrown away, and the symbols of freedom — Trees of Liberty — planted by the delivered Jews. Their enthusiasm at the great transformation was boundless. For the first time in the history of Italian Jewry the commander of a victorious army appeared not as an oppressor but as a liberator of the Jewish people.

Bonaparte himself led the army into the city of Ancona. There the Jews had found themselves in acute danger, for they were suspected of being engaged in a plot to supply the French with arms; a house-to-house search was made in the ghetto, several persons were arrested, and the Jewish quarter was beleaguered by an angry mob. In this very critical moment the French entered the city. Strangely enough, a number of Jewish soldiers were among the first to arrive. They came as saviors, causing the mobs to melt away. They led the march of liberation into the ghetto, tearing the yellow badge from the heads of the Jews and replacing it by a tricolor rosette. Small wonder that this rescue appeared to many as a divine miracle and was described as such by an eye-witness in a Hebrew chronicle. On this occasion the first Jewish Napoleonic legend was born: Bonaparte was welcomed by virtue of a Hebrew translation of his name as *ḥelek tov*, *i.e.*, "Good Portion," thus being made a figure of almost Messianic qualities.[12] On St. Helena, Napoleon referred to them in a memorable passage of his Memoirs: "Les Juifs, nombreux à Ancône, aussi que les Mahométans d'Albanie et de Grèce, y étaient soumis à d'anciens usages humiliants et contraires aux droits de l'hospitalité. Un des premiers soins de Napoléon fut les en affranchir."

The liberation of the Jews of Venice, Verona, and Padua by Bonaparte during his first Italian campaign was unfortunately followed by a cruel interlude which reversed their situation and exposed them to persecutions. The temporary relapse of the Jews into their previous state, and the atrocities which they had to endure by angry mobs, were the outcome of the infamous treaty of Campo Formio in which Venice and the greater part of her territory were handed over to Austria, and of Bonaparte's decision to embark upon the Egyptian adventure. It took another Italian campaign and the battle of Austerlitz in order to restore their rights and to let them enjoy the benefits of a tolerant regime. Their second deliverance increased their affection toward him to such a degree that it bordered on adoration. The "ḥelek tov" became in the eyes of the Italian Jews the *ohev Israel*, "Lover of Israel." Tributes were paid to him in prose and verse, both Hebrew and Italian. The words were confirmed by actions. Jews enrolled in the militia, in the National Guards, and in Napoleon's army. Many of them lost their lives in his campaigns. The legend survives of how on the retreat from Moscow the Italian Jewish soldiers sang Hebrew psalms round the campfire to the tune of the Marseillaise.

As to Bonaparte, the impact of his first encounter with the Jewish population on his subsequent attitude to the Jewish people and to the nationalities of the Levant, which he met almost immediately after the Italian campaign, can hardly be underestimated. In fact, this encounter was one of the experiences which shaped the pattern of the Expedition to Egypt and the Near East. The lessons learned in Italy were to be applied to Africa and Asia.

PART TWO

BONAPARTE'S EASTERN EXPEDITION AND THE GENESIS OF HIS PROCLAMATION TO THE JEWISH NATION

3

THE ORIGIN OF THE EASTERN EXPEDITION

The landing of the French armada on the Egyptian shores
marked the moment when the decomposition of the Ottoman
Empire had become irreversible. The rise of modern Egypt
begins with the battle of the Pyramids, and the Eastern
Question has, from that moment on, never ceased to be one
of the dominant issues of international politics. The uninten-
tional consequences of the Expedition were of no less historic
significance. It was from the pursuit and finally the destruction of the French fleet by Nelson that England's prepon-
derance in the Mediterranean dates. With the British suc-
ceeding Bonaparte in the possession of Malta, the epoch of
England's commanding influence in the Middle East was initiated. The effects of the Expedition on human civilization
proved immeasurable. The science of Egyptology was born
when the savants of the Institut d'Egypte began their re-
searches in Cairo. The building of the Suez Canal, one of
the declared aims of the Expedition, remained from then on-
ward *the* project of the French nation, until it became a
reality through the ingenuity of Ferdinand de Lesseps. Thus,
the Expedition may rightly be described as a definite step
in uniting the Orient with the Western world.

François Charles-Roux, the historian of Bonaparte's Expedition to Egypt, has shown that the Eastern campaign was one of the most frequently discussed and proposed projects in French history.[13] Not the suggestions of the diplomats and statesmen nor the favorable general trend nor even the conflict with England would have led to the realization of the adventurous campaign, if the idea had not crystallized in the mind of young Napoleon Bonaparte. A plan for the conquest of the eastern Mediterranean was conceived by Bonaparte in Venice. Two letters written on August 16, 1797, contain an illuminating outline of this epoch-making program. "We would in vain aim at the preservation of the Turkish Empire," he wrote to Talleyrand, "We shall see its fall within our lifetime... The fanaticism of liberty that has already begun to make itself felt in Greece will become more powerful than religious fanaticism. The great nation France will find there more friends than the Russians." A simultaneous letter to the Directory closed with the sudden and unprecedented statement: "It will not be long before we realize that, if we are effectively to destroy England, we must get hold of Egypt." In that hour, the Expedition to Egypt was born. The expansion of France and the destruction of England's supremacy were combined with his plan to bring about a national movement in the Near East. The same broad outlook is reflected in the words he addressed to the army in Ancona in February, 1797: "Soldiers, for the first time, the flag of France floats over the eastern shore of the Adriatic, only twenty-four leagues from Alexander the Great's point of departure for the East. The same glorious destiny awaits you."

4

ANTECEDENT AND CONTEMPORARY TRENDS
TOWARD THE RESTORATION OF THE JEWS

In the years and very days preceding the start of Napoleon's Expedition the fate of Palestine had become the object of a public discussion in connection with the problem of the restoration of the Jews to their ancient homeland. This fact may be surprising to those who still ignore the important part which the Jewish and non-Jewish movements played long before the rise of political Zionism.[14] In the British Isles a continuous and steadily growing movement for the Restoration of the Jews had been in progress since the end of the Elizabethan era. The expectation of this apocalyptic event constituted an element of the Puritan revolution and had developed into a theological doctrine. The adherents of this doctrine believed that according to certain prophecies and the Revelation of St. John the dispersed Jews, together with the lost tribes, would be — in a converted state — restored to the Promised Land. In 1589, Francis Kett had been condemned and burnt alive for adhering to this belief, then considered heretical. In 1621 Sir Henry Finch dealt with the subject in a comprehensive treatise, *The World's Great Restauration or the Calling of the Jews and [with Them] of All the Nations and Kingdoms of the Earth to the Faith of*

Christ. In 1640, the year in which the Great Rebellion began, the suppressed doctrine was vigorously revived. The millenarianism of the Puritan Commonwealth provided most fertile soil for the ideas of the doctrine. The momentous political event in the Jewish history of those days, the readmission of the Jews to England, was also closely linked with the movement for the Restoration of the Jews, as is clearly shown by Manasseh Ben Israel's "Hope of Israel."

John Milton, the greatest representative of "English Hebraism," dealt with the question in an admirable way in his *Paradise Regained.* Isaac Newton and William Whiston, the mathematician and theologian who succeeded Newton to the chair of Mathematics at Cambridge, enriched the doctrine with new interpretations, and David Hartley, a well-known physician and philosopher in the middle of the eighteenth century, incorporated the doctrine of the Restoration of the Jews in his *Observations on Man.* In 1747, the first book dealing with the question without a conversionist tendency which until then had constituted an integral part of the doctrine, was published: S. Collet's *Treatise on the Future Restoration of the Jews and Israelites to Their Own Land.* But this rather academic treatment of the Restorationist doctrine was transformed, after the outbreak of the French Revolution, into a political activity. History seemed to have assumed apocalyptic proportions, with one kingdom after another being broken up and institutions believed immutable exposed to shattering blows. It had indeed become difficult for students of prophecies *not* to find references to these happenings in Daniel or the Revelation.

In 1790, Richard Beere, Rector of Sudbroke, made a memorable attempt — the first of its kind — to influence English foreign policy in favor of the restoration of the Jews by addressing a letter to William Pitt. The writer announced the impending publication of a pamphlet dealing with "the final restoration of the Jews to the Holy Land" which "was to commence according to the Holy Scripture in the ensuing year," *i.e.,* 1791. Beere appealed to Pitt to "bring about this great event," and implored him "not to disarm until a universal peace can be established over all Europe."[15]

This scarcely noted episode was, however, soon followed by a far more sensational event which in an odd and grotesque way seemed to foreshadow later happenings within Bonaparte's career. The hero of this fantastic story was Richard Brothers, a British naval officer who, probably influenced by Quaker teachings, had on one occasion refused to take an oath and was punished by the docking of pay and imprisonment. This sad experience produced in Brothers' unbalanced mind a state of exaltation. His personal conflict with the world became identified with the stormy events on the international scene. The year was 1792. The French army marched into Flanders and threatened Holland. A year later Louis XVI died on the scaffold. By February, 1793, England was at war with Revolutionary France. Throughout that time of tense excitement Brothers lived in his poor home in Paddington, entirely absorbed by the composition of his *opus mysticum.* It appeared in 1794 under the incredible title:

A Revealed Knowledge of the Prophecies and Times, Wrote under the direction of the Lord God and published by His sacred command. It being the First sign of Warning for the benefit of all nations containing with other Great and Remarkable Things, Not Revealed to any other Person of Earth, the Restoration of the Hebrew to Jerusalem by the Year of 1798 under their revealed Prince and Prophet.

A second part, published in the same year, was entitled:

Second sign of Warning for the benefit of all Nations by the Man that will be revealed to the Hebrews as their Prince and Prophet.

Quoting copiously from the Bible, Brothers endeavored to prove that the French Revolution was the calamity foretold by Scriptures, and therefore must succeed. War against France was hopeless, indeed suicidal. The Millennium and the restoration of the Hebrews to Palestine were imminent. He, Richard Brothers, as descendant of James, "the Brother of our Lord" — thus a "Nephew of the Almighty" — had been divinely appointed to lead the Hebrews back to their land. On July 1 he would reach Constantinople on his way to Zion, and the restoration would be accomplished by 1798. It would embrace the "visible Hebrews" as well as the "invisible Hebrews" — descendants of the ten tribes scattered among the nations, chiefly members of the English nation.[16]

Countless copies of the pamphlet, *Revealed Knowledge*, were sold. Edition followed edition; it was reprinted in Ireland and America, and a French edition appeared in Paris in 1796. The predictions of the insane author, as far as the military achievements of the revolutionary army were concerned, had literally come true. France had conquered all her enemies, and was continuing her victorious march. Thus the book of the Englishman presumably found many readers in France. We may be entitled to assume that the predictions of Brothers concerning the restoration of the Hebrews were remembered in 1798, when the young Napoleon Bonaparte was about to set out for the Orient. There is no direct evidence that he himself was acquainted with the prophecies of Brothers, but Bonaparte was eager to gather all available information about historical and political events which were related to his own activities.

The voice of the British Movement for the Restoration of the Jews was, by no means, an isolated phenomenon. The idea of the restoration of the Jews had found its expression on the European continent since the middle of the seventeenth century. The millenarian wave which had swept over England in the 1740s was accompanied by a similar, though less consistent, trend in various European countries where the Thirty Years' War was approaching its climax and creating an atmosphere pregnant with eschatological expectations. In different corners of Europe, mystical enthusiasts advocated the idea of Israel's impending return and revival.[17]

The religious eschatological element declined in the eighteenth century and was replaced by rationalistic trends of thought; the total identification with biblical personages and events was superseded by the consideration of economic, geographic, and historical factors. Restoration became for some thinkers a political goal justified by utilitarian, and later, by humanitarian reasons.

Charles-Joseph Prince de Ligne (1735–1814), born in Brussels, friend of Voltaire and Rousseau, a favorite of the Austrian emperor's and of Catherine of Russia, one of the most

lucid minds of his age, drew up the most advanced scheme
for the Restoration of the Jewish people conceived until
then.[18] De Ligne sought the basis for the reestablishment of
the Jewish State in negotiations to be conducted with the
Sultan. He suggested that the Jews themselves, namely those
resident in Turkey, should be the mediators. De Ligne's
Mémoire sur les Juifs was published in 1797. Its appearance
coincided thus with the moment when Bonaparte conceived
the idea of an expedition to the East. Whether he became
acquainted with de Ligne's *Mémoire* can, of course, be only
a matter of conjecture, though some circumstances lend a
certain amount of probability to such an assumption. De
Ligne admired Napoleon, published in 1807 an appreciative
essay about him under the title "Ma Napoléonide," and took
care to pass his works to the French Emperor. One may,
therefore, suppose that — after the treaty of Campo Formio
— he may have made Bonaparte the liberator of the Italian
Jews, acquainted with his ideas about the deliverance of the
Jewish people.

While it is difficult to decide which of the ideas, predictions, and plans conceived in England or France about
Israel's revival actually reached Bonaparte before he left for
the East, there can hardly be any doubt that he had not
missed a most clear pre-Zionist voice sounded in his immediate proximity and almost in the very hour of his departure. Moreover, this voice was addressed to him from a
very familiar corner: It came from the midst of Italian Jewry.
Within the framework of an anonymous "Letter to the
Brethren" an elaborate plan for the restoration of the Jewish
people was drawn up.

The writer of the "Letter" pointed out that the hatred of the nation toward the Jews had not abated. The yoke resting on their shoulders would be lifted only when they had regained their rank as a nation among other nations of the world. For the realization of this hope the author of the "Letter" turned to "the invincible nation which now fills the world with her glory." The author proposed the establishment of a council, to be elected by all Jews in accordance with a carefully pre-pared scheme. The council was to conduct negotiations with the Directory of France through an appointed agent about the restoration of a Jewish commonwealth. The "Letter" closed with a passionate appeal:

> O my Brethren, what sacrifices ought we not make to attain this object? We shall return to our country, we shall live under our own laws — we shall behold those places where our ancestors demonstrated their courage and their virtues. Already I see you all animated with a holy zeal. Israelites! the end of our misfortune is at hand. The opportunity is favorable — take care that you do not allow it to escape!

The "Letter" aroused special interest in Britain. On June 19, 1798, the *Courier de Londres* reproduced the appeal in full; shortly afterward the same periodical published a special edition. More significant still was the publication of the "Letter" by the semi-official *St. James' Chronicle* on July 14, 1798, when Bonaparte was already in Egypt. The feature of this reprint was a significant divergence from the Italian text. While the latter contains the appeal, "O my brethren, let us rebuild the temple of Jerusalem!" the English paper quotes this passage as follows: "...let us reestablish the Empire of Jerusalem!" A strict translation from the Italian appeared in the widely circulated literary magazine, *The Monthly Visitor and Pocket Companion* under the title: "Letters recently written from a Jew to his Brethren, concerning the establishment of a new Jewish Republic" (vol. IV, p. 383–386).

In France itself the leading literary magazine, *La décade philosophique, littéraire et politique,* quoted the "Letter" in an article published under the heading "Economie sociale. Suite des considérations sur l'Egypte et la Syrie." The conviction was expressed that the Jews would support Palestine with men and gold. "They will come in crowds not only to make industry flourish, but also to defray the cost of the revolution in Syria and Egypt." The article appeared in the issues no. 20/21, year VI, 20 and 30 Germinal (April 9 and 19, 1798), practically on the eve of the Expedition which started less than a month later. Even if Bonaparte had not become acquainted with the "Letter" itself (although it is probable that its author tooks steps to bring his scheme to the notice of official quarters), he would have seen it on the pages of *La décade.* The article was one of the last messages which Bonaparte received before he left France in order to bring about "the revolution of Egypt and Syria." Future events were to prove how deeply it had been impressed upon his memory.

5

THE EXPEDITION TO EGYPT AND ITS JEWISH ELEMENTS

On May 19, 1798, an armada of 55 warships and about 300 ships of all kinds, carrying a landing force of 43,000, under the command of Napoleon Bonaparte, began to move out of the harbor of Toulon. Four square miles of the sea were covered by the huge fleet — the greatest seen in the Mediterranean since the days of the Crusades. The destination of the armada had been kept a secret almost till the last moment. Only the members of the Directory and Bonaparte's entourage were aware of it. This secrecy and a favourable wind enabled Bonaparte to reach the first goal of the voyage — Malta. The seizure of the important Mediterranean island had been contemplated by Bonaparte from the outset, and it was foreseen by the Directory in a special decree.

The French occupation brought to an end one of the most humiliating chapters in Jewish history. Jews had lived on the island since the days of the Romans, though their numbers were never considerable. In 1553 the Knights of St. John took Malta from Spain and transformed it into an impregnable fortress of Christian Europe. The knights enslaved Jewish prisoners, and mercilessly used or sold them. The cruel fate of the Jews had moved Joseph Nasi, Duke of Naxos, in

the sixteenth century, and the Jews of England and other
Jewish communities in the eighteenth, to intervene on behalf
of their unhappy brethren and to raise funds for their ran-
som. Bonaparte's arrival brought freedom to the Jewish
slaves still living on the island. Slavery was expressly abolished. Moreover, in the constitution which Bonaparte drew
up for Malta provision was made permitting Jews to have
synagogues. Thus, the re-creation of a Jewish community on
Malta was initiated by Bonaparte.[19] On June 19, Bonaparte's
armada left Malta. He could no longer conceal the destination of the voyage from the army and decided to inform the
soldiers of his aims. The proclamation which he drew up
contains the political program of the Expedition and a manual
of discipline for the army. It is addressed to the Army of
the Orient and dated the 4th Messidor, year VI (June 22,
1798):

> *Soldiers!*
>
> *You are about to undertake a conquest whose effects
> on the world's civilization and trade are incalculable.*
>
> *You will inflict upon England a blow which is certain
> to wound her in her most sensitive spot, while waiting
> for the day when you can deal her the death blow.*
>
> *We shall make some wearisome marches; we shall fight
> a few battles; we shall succeed in all our enterprises;
> destiny is for us.*
>
> *The Mameluke beys, who exclusively favor English
> trade, who have oppressed our merchants with vexa-
> tions, and who are tyrannizing over the unhappy people
> of the Nile valley, will cease to exist a few days after*

our landing. The people with whom we shall live are Mohammedans. Their chief creed is this: "There is no God but God, and Mohammed is His prophet."

Do not contradict them. Act toward them as in the past you have acted toward the Jews and the Italians. Respect their muftis and imams, as you have respected the rabbis and the bishops.

Show the same tolerance toward the ceremonies prescribed by the Koran and toward the mosques as you have shown toward convents and synagogues, toward the religions of Moses and of Jesus Christ.

The Roman legions used to protect all religions. You will find here customs quite different from those of Europe; you must become used to them.

The people of the countries where we are going treat their women differently from the way we do; but, in all countries, the man who rapes a woman is a monster.

Looting enriches but a few. It dishonors us, it destroys our resources, and it turns the people whom we want to befriend into our enemies.

The first city we shall see was built by Alexander. At every step we shall find traces of deeds worthy of being emulated by the French.[20]

The emphasis laid on the treatment of the Jews is striking; Bonaparte refers to them four times. Jews are first linked with Italians and thus viewed as a nation rather than as a religious community. In naming them Bonaparte indicated the importance which he ascribed to them and to the attitude shown them.

Translated into Arabic, the proclamation was printed in
thousands of copies before the landing of the armada. On
July 1, 1798, Bonaparte set foot on Egyptian soil. The next
day, Alexandria was taken by storm. A few days later, with
the armada under the command of vice-admiral Brueys, apparently safely anchored, Bonaparte set the army in motion
toward Cairo. After an ordeal of fatigue and privation the
army sighted the Pyramids and the Mameluke army. Six thousand mounted Mamelukes were gathered there, joined by
hosts of Bedouin and fellahin, altogether about thirty thousand men. Bonaparte ordered the formation of five impenet-
rable squares and awaited the attack of the glittering enemy.
Before the sun set the reign of the Mamelukes had come to an
end. Leaving behind 2000 dead soldiers and 400 camels, their
leaders retreated with the remainder of their army. Bonaparte entered Cairo triumphantly and made his headquarters
in the imposing palace Ezbekyeh. It was one of the proudest
days of his career.

Catastrophe, like in a Greek tragedy, struck almost immediately afterward. Nelson, after having searched the Mediterranean for weeks, discovered the French fleet off Alexandria.
The Battle of the Nile on August 1 and 2 brought about the
almost total annihilation of the French armada. The disaster
seemed to have doomed the Expedition. The army was cut
off from France, and Egypt subjected to a tight blockade;
the exchange of letters between Bonaparte and the Directory
was cut off. Thus, whatever Bonaparte's original intentions
might have been, unalterable necessity forced upon him the
threefold task of rebuilding Egypt, of securing his position
by an advance toward the East, and of consolidating the

Levant as a springboard to the Turkish capital or to India.

There was no more urgent, or difficult, task before Bonaparte than of gaining the confidence of the native population. A *Divan Général* of 189 notables was established in Cairo as the first step to self-government and was invested with consultative functions. Bonaparte took great care to observe the customs and fashions of the inhabitants. The experienced Venture de Paradis was his constant and most reliable guide in this respect. Helped by Venture's interpretations, Bonaparte engaged in discussions with the muftis and the mullahs, and professed himself a friend of Islam and admirer of "Allah, His Prophet and of the Koran." Negotiations with the muftis were inaugurated to grant Bonaparte a *Fetwa*, an order of the highest Mohammedan authorities to take an oath of allegiance to his regime. In fact, he succeeded in obtaining from Mecca a modified *Fetwa* which dispensed him and the French from the cardinal conditions of the conversion to Islam; circumcision and abstention from wine-drinking, under the provision of setting aside for charity one fifth of the income in place of the customary tenth. Bonaparte accepted the terms and, in addition, promised to build in Egypt a mosque of unparalleled beauty and size. Wearing a turban, surrounded by native counselors, accommodating his language and style of behavior to Egyptian standards, Bonaparte assumed the appearance of an Oriental ruler.

The ostentatious signs of favor shown to the Mohammedan population and the inclination of Bonaparte to Islam could not sway the allegiance of the people toward the French invader and worse still, prevent the growth of mistrust and unrest. When a new house impost was laid upon the city, an insurrection broke out on October 21 and assumed dangerous proportions. Dupuy, the military governor of the capital, was stabbed to death by an Arab; parts of Cairo were seized by the insurgents; residences of officers were stormed and their occupants massacred. Only when Bonaparte put his heavy guns into action did he succeed in suppressing the revolt.

Shocking and disillusioning as the experience was, Bonaparte did not change his policy toward the Muslims. An amnesty was proclaimed and a new Divan constituted. Nevertheless, the event could not but shatter the confidence Bonaparte and his entourage had put in the Muslims and, at the same time, raise the trust in the non-Mohammedan part of the population which had abstained from participating in the revolt. The Copts — the predominant Christian sect — obtained liberty and equality with the coming of Bonaparte. An order was issued by Bonaparte to recruit among "the Greeks" (the Copts) men for three companies, each of one hundred men.

The Jewish community of Egypt, and of Cairo in particular, formed another important part of the non-Mohammedan population. There had been, only few decades before Bonaparte's arrival in Egypt, an anti-Jewish riot in Cairo which brought total destruction upon the *Harat Yehoudos* (Jewish Quarter). Although they had sided with the Muslim population, the leaders of the community did their best to remain neutral during the foreign occupation. The economic importance of Jewish merchants of Cairo invested the community with some authority.

Bonaparte continued toward the Jews of Egypt the policy

he had inaugurated in Italy. He took care to bestow upon the Jewish community a status by which it officially acquired equality with other religious denominations. In fact, he showed a special confidence in the Jews by sanctioning the organization they had themselves created. It was the first statute given to a Jewish community outside of Europe. An even more momentous act was the appointment, on September 7, 1798, of two "high priests of the Jewish nation" *grand-prêtres de la nation juive* in the persons of Sabbato Adda and Tolbi di Figura. Bonaparte followed in the footsteps of Alexander who had granted the Egyptian Jews extensive privileges. Moreover, the title he had chosen for the Jewish dignitaries, "high priests," indicates that it was his intention to renew the ancient high office. Although out of tune with the sublime character of the sacred Hebrew institution, the act was in accordance with Bonaparte's revivalist tendencies. The most revealing part of the *Ordre* was, however, the use of the denomination "Jewish Nation." It was the first instance in Napoleon Bonaparte's dealings with the Jews in which he himself used this expression.

Bonaparte again used this expression on a visit to the famous and ancient Greek Orthodox monastery of St. Catherine at Mount Sinai. He decided to bestow upon the monks a unique grant of privileges by special order of December 19, 1798, which opened as follows:

> Bonaparte, General-in-Chief, wishing to favor the convent at Mount Sinai —
> 1st. In order to transmit to future races the traditions of our conquest;

2nd. Through respect for Moses and the Jewish nation, whose cosmogony retraces the earliest ages;

3rd. Because the convent of Mount Sinai is inhabited by well-educated and refined men, living in the midst of the barbarity of the desert;

Orders, &, &,"

A few days after the signing of the order to the monastery, Bonaparte, in the company of a carefully selected group, was on the way to the Sinai peninsula, to discover the walls of Moses. But the excursion into the Sinai peninsula proved to be only a short prelude to a new decisive phase of the Expedition. News which awaited Bonaparte confirmed beyond any doubt that Turkey had declared war upon France and that Jazzar Pasha, the governor of Acre, had been commissioned to march on Egypt. The invasion of the Holy Land had become unavoidable.

6

FROM THE PYRAMIDS TO MOUNT TABOR

In a letter addressed to the Directory on February 10, 1799, immediately before the start of his operations, Bonaparte described his three aims: "firstly, to assure the conquest of Egypt by constructing a stronghold beyond the desert...; secondly, to oblige the Porte to explain itself, and thereby support the negotiations that you have doubtless set on foot...; thirdly, to deprive the English fleet of the supplies that it draws from Syria, by employing the two remaining months of winter so as to make all that coast friendly to me through war and negotiations."

Bonaparte's intention of extending French power across the Middle East was in accordance with his program as it had been outlined in the letter to the Directory. No exact geographical description of the "stronghold beyond the desert" which Bonaparte was going to establish, was given. Acre, Damascus, or even farther advanced outposts could suit this indication. As to the task he set himself of making "all that coast friendly through war and negotiations," an enforced or peaceful settlement with Jazzar fitted such a purpose as did a restoration of the Jewish nation. There occurs, in fact, in the same important programmatic letter to the Directory a passage which appears to be a hint of Bonapart's restorationist intentions.

> ...Ibrahim Pasha, Abdullah Pasha and the other pashas are at Gaza, and menace Egypt with an invasion. I leave within an hour in order to meet them. It will be necessary to cross the desert without water in nine days. I have assembled considerable numbers of camels and I hope that I shall lack nothing. When you read this letter, it is quite possible that I shall be standing on the ruins of the city of Solomon...

Bonaparte left Cairo on February 10, 1799. During the crossing of the desert, everyone was aware of its historic significance. While some compared Bonaparte with St. Louis who in 1250 had landed with 40,000 men in Egypt, and then, after having been taken prisoner and ransomed, proceeded to Acre and stayed in Palestine until 1252, others felt that Bonaparte and his men followed in the footsteps of Moses and of the Children of Israel. As the troops paused at the cairn marking the frontier of Palestine and Egypt, they broke out spontaneously into the national hymn. Biblical comparisons of this kind and identifications with Israel's past became a standing feature of the Syrian campaign. As the army was encamped on the ruins of the ancient cities, the Holy Scriptures were read aloud in the tent of the General-in-Chief.[21]

The events of the campaign unfolded themselves with dramatic speed. El Arish was taken on February 20. The garrison capitulated and was released on condition that the men

would not take part in the war. On February 25 abandoned
Gaza was occupied. Five days later the army seized Ramleh.
In his memoirs, Napoleon reported the army's eagerness to
enter Jerusalem, with the characteristic detail that some of
the older soldiers were chanting psalms and Jeremiah's lam-
entations.[22]

But it seems that Napoleon in an early stage of the campaign changed his original intention. According to his aide,
Louis-Antonini Bourrienne, his reasons were strictly strategic. At Ramleh he asked the Commander-in-Chief whether
he did not intend to march on Jerusalem. Bonaparte's answer
to this questions is related in detail:

> Oh no! Jerusalem is not in my line of operations. I do
> not wish to be annoyed by mountaineers on difficult
> roads. And, besides, on the other side of the mountains
> I would be assailed by swarms of cavalry. I have no
> ambitions for the fate of Cassius.[23]

Other considerations might also have been relevant. The capture of Jerusalem would not have been merely a military
event. The highest prize of the campaign was not to be occupied without certainty of holding it indefinitely.

The French advanced along the coast and stormed Jaffa on
March 7, massacring four thousand soldiers and a large part
of the inhabitants. The Jewish population of Jaffa, too, suffered great losses. Bonaparte himself became entangled in
Jaffa in a crime which is regarded as one of the blackest of his
career. A group of almost 2,300 Turks who had barricaded
themselves and fired from a caravan, was saved by Croisier,
Bonaparte's aide-de-camp, from the enraged soldiery by ac-

cepting their offer to lay down their arms. A court-martial, after having deliberated for three days, pronounced a death penalty upon all the prisoners; Bonaparte then ordered the execution of the prisoners which took place on March 10.

In Jaffa, Bonaparte also withstood the supreme test of self-sacrifice. During the short stay, the plague struck the expeditionary army for the first time. An insufficient number of doctors was at hand and many soldiers shrank from lifting a comrade to a stretcher. The morale of the army was restored by Bonaparte who sat by the sufferers and raised a dying victim with his own hands. When Napoleon's chief of staff Berthier protested against such imprudence, Bonaparte, walking to another bed, replied: "I am but doing my duty."

Despite all these tragic and ominous events, Jaffa was an important stepping stone. There Bonaparte set up a provisional government for Palestine with Jacques-François Menou as governor-general, helped by divans established in Gaza, Ramleh, and Jaffa after the Egyptian pattern. To the sheikhs, ulamas, and the inhabitants of these cities, a proclamation was addressed on March 9, couched in terms similar to a previous proclamation (of February 24, 1799) to the dignitaries of Gaza. It emphatically put the blame for the invasion of Palestine on Jazzar who had extended his reign of terror beyond his *pashalik* and sent troops to El Arish. Bonaparte assured the people that the administration of justice by the *kadis* would be maintained and religion protected and respected. The striking Mohammedan coloring, so distinctive in the proclamation to the inhabitants of Egypt, was conspicuously absent. The proclamation closed with a warning:

You shall bear in mind that all human efforts against
me are useless, for whatever I undertake must succeed.
Those who declare themselves my friends prosper.
Those who declare themselves my enemies perish. The
recent example of Jaffa and Gaza must have taught you
that I am terrible against my enemies, but good to my
friends, and particularly mild and merciful toward poor
people.

From the headquarters in Jaffa Bonaparte addressed a proclamation (on March 9) to the sheikhs, ulamas, and the commander of Jerusalem. It was a shortened version of the proclamation to Gaza, Ramleh, and Jaffa linked with an invitation to send delegates to offer peaceful submission. Bonaparte
gave instructions to General Régnier in a special covering
letter, dated March 9, 1799, which contains the following
passage:

You will find enclosed, Citizen General, a letter to the
inhabitants of Jerusalem; have eight to ten copies made,
and send them by different channels; one of them may
arrive. The General Staff is also sending you a proclamation to the population of Palestine, give it the widest
distribution possible...

Although Bourrienne declared that no answer was received,
other sources testify to the success of the proclamation. According to one narrative, not only the Turkish commander
of Jerusalem hurried to Jaffa to profess his neutrality, but
behind a Christian deputation there was "a company of Jews
who spoke of the Commander-in-Chief as the second Messiah."[24] As a matter of fact, the heads of the Jewish com-

munity in Jerusalem remained loyal to the Turkish government and helped fortify the city against the invading army.[25]

Bonaparte, on the eve of his further advance, might have felt that a great part of Palestine was firmly in his hands, and that a part of the Jewish population had rallied behind him. Triumphantly he reported in his closing sentence of a letter to the Directory of March 13: "The army of the Republic is the mistress of the whole of Palestine." But there is further documentary proof of Bonaparte's conviction that a permanently pacified Palestine was about to emerge. In a letter of March 10, he urged Poussielgue, the economic administrator of Egypt, to encourage the merchants of Damietta and Cairo to come to Jaffa in order to sell their rice and to buy oil and soap of which there was plenty in Palestine. Everything should be done for the encouragement of commerce between the two countries. In the same letter he gave the order to propagate copies of the proclamation to the population of Palestine by all means and expressly asked that 2,000 reprints be sent to Damietta and Alexandria, to the Levant and to the Barbary Coast, and to Constantinople, as well.

Bonaparte knew, however, that the conquest of Palestine was not completed as long as Acre was in the hands of the enemy. The formidable opposition Bonaparte met from the forces allied against him soon became manifest. They succeeded in intercepting French vessels carrying new guns and siege artillery, and put them to effective use against the besiegers; British warship were able to develop flanking fire on the French batteries. Despite the initial setbacks, Bonaparte felt confident that the fortress would soon fall. Ten

days after the arrival at Acre, on March 28, he issued orders
for a general assault, but the attempt to storm a tower dam-
aged by field artillery failed. Another general assault undertaken on April 1, though more costly in casualties, was not
more successful. The two failures to take the fortress by a
coup de main did not discourage Bonaparte and his generals,
but rather taught them that heavy artillery was needed. Bonaparte took advantage of a comparative lull in the fighting
to strengthen his position in the country. A deputation of
the Motouêly tribe consisting of eight chiefs was received
by him and each of them was presented with a fur coat. "The
country is for us," Bonaparte declared in a letter of April 5
to General Degua. "What we need is only the city [Acre] of
which we hope to be in possession soon."

At that very moment a menace more serious than any-
thing he had encountered during the Syrian campaign appeared. An army of nearly 30,000 containing infantry and
mounted troops, hastened from Damascus for the relief of
Acre. The army advanced to the Plain of Esdraelon (Jezreel), a move which clearly threatened communications between Acre and Jaffa. A decisive battle had to be waged.
It was fought in the Plain of Esdraelon, not far from the foot
of Mount Tabor. There Kléber's division of 2,000 men was
hard pressed for some hours by a motley array drawn from
diverse parts of the Sultan's dominions. At last Bonaparte's
cannon was heard; marching swiftly on with his troops drawn
up in three squares, he speedily brushed aside the enveloping
clouds of Orientals; finally, by well-combined efforts, the
French hurled back the enemy toward mountain passes, some
of which had been seized due to the commander's foresight.

At the close of this memorable day (April 10) an army of
nearly 30,000 had been completely routed by the valor and
skillful operations of less than a seventh of that number.
No battle of modern times more closely resembles the ex-
ploits of Alexander than this masterly concentration of force
and firepower. Kléber exclaimed as he met and embraced
the commander on the field of battle: "General, how great
you are!"

7

THE ISSUE OF THE PROCLAMATION TO THE JEWISH NATION

After the battle, Bonaparte climbed to the summit of Mount Tabor and had a view of the land filled with sacred memories — memories of other great battles decisive in the history of Israel. It was here that Barak the son of Abinoam, summoned by Deborah the prophetess, had utterly defeated Sisera, the captain of Jabin, in the first war of Israel's independence. This indeed was the spot glorified in Deborah's Song:

> *The kings came, they fought;*
> *Then fought the kings of Canaan,*
> *In Taanach by the waters of Megiddo;*
> *They took no gain of money.*
> *They fought from heaven,*
> *The stars in their courses fought against Sisera,*
> *The brook Kishon swept them away,*
> *The ancient brook, the brook Kishon.*

Judges 5: 19—21

Here Gideon won his glorious victory over the allied forces of the Midianites and the Amalekites and all the children of the East who "lay along in the valley like locusts for multitude" (Judges 7:12). Then the mountains surrounding the valley resounded with the cries: "For the Lord and for Gideon!" (Judges 7:18).

Bonaparte, whose mind was always inclined to view the present in the mirror of ancient history, was probably aware of the analogy between these great biblical encounters and his own victory. This battle, fought in the neighborhood of the biblical Megiddo — the Armageddon of Rev. 16:16 — with all the consequences which it seemed to imply for the outcome of the whole Eastern campaign, could not fail to inspire incredible visions.

Everything seemed, in those spring days, to be turning in Bonaparte's favor. Even before he returned to the camp before Acre, the news arrived that some heavy artillery had safely reached Jaffa. In only a few days these invaluable weapons were to arrive before Acre on the secure land route. The final assault on the fortress was therefore imminent. The fortress was at his mercy, its fall within his grasp. On April 19 (the day before the issue of the Proclamation) Bonaparte wrote four letters to Cairo in which the fall of Acre within the very next days was stated to be inevitable. The prospect of Acre's imminent fall also made Bonaparte conceive new plans. Bourriene, his old comrade and secretary, has recorded a conversation which, although it took place on May 8, reflects ideas born immediately after the battle at Mount Tabor. Vast hopes and fantastic schemes arose in Bonaparte's mind:

> If I succeed, as I expect, I shall find in the town the Pasha's treasures and arms for 300,000 men. I will stir

up the people of Syria who, as you know, pray for his destruction at every assault. I shall then march upon Damascus and Aleppo. On advancing into the country, the discontented will flock round my standard and swell my army. I will announce to the people the abolition of servitude and of the tyrannical government of the Pashas. I shall arrive at Constantinople with large masses of soldiery. I shall overturn the Turkish Empire, which will fix my name in the records of posterity.[26]

In a passage of his memoirs about the Egyptian and Syrian campaigns he stated: "Had St. Jean d'Acre fallen, I would have changed the face of the world."

An extraordinary passage occurs in the memoirs in which these details have been recorded:

The Jews in Syria were fairly numerous; they were moved by a vague hope: a rumor was current among them that Napoleon, *after taking Acre* [my italics], would go to Jerusalem and that he wanted to restore Solomon's temple.[27]

After the annihilation of the army which was supposed to relieve Acre, with the certain prospect that the fortress would fall within the next days, he felt entitled to anticipate the capture of Acre as well as of Jerusalem and to regard himself as master of Palestine. The time was ripe for his other plans. Four days after the victory at Mount Tabor, on the day after the arrival of the auxiliary artillery on April 20, 1799, Bonaparte issued his Proclamation to the Jewish Nation.

PART THREE

BONAPARTE'S ATTEMPT TO RESTORE THE JEWISH NATION

8

THE PROCLAMATION AND THE COVERING LETTER

General Headquarters, Ierusalem
1st Floréal in the year 7 of the
French Republic (April 20, 1799)

Bonaparte, Commander-in-Chief of the Armies of the French Republic in Africa and Asia, to the Rightful Heirs of Palestine.

Israelites, unique nation, whom, in thousands of years, lust of conquest and tyranny were able to deprive of the ancestral lands only, but not of name and national existence!

Attentive and impartial observers of the destinies of nations, even though not endowed with the gifts of seers like Isaiah and Joel, have also felt long since what these, with beautiful and uplifting faith, foretold when they saw the approaching destruction of their kingdom and fatherland: that the ransomed of the Lord shall return, and come with singing unto Zion, and the enjoyment of henceforth undisturbed possession of their heritage will send an everlasting joy upon their heads (Isaiah 35:10).

Arise then, with gladness, ye exiled! A war unexampled in the annals of history, waged in self-defense by a nation whose hereditary lands were regarded by her enemies as plunder to be divided, arbitrarily and at their convenience, by a stroke of the pen of Cabinets, avenges her own shame and the shame of the remotest nations, long forgotten under the yoke of slavery, and, too, the almost two-thousand-year-old ignominy put upon you; and while time and circumstances would seem to be least favorable to a restatement of your claims or even to their expression, and indeed to be compelling their complete abandonment, she (France) offers to you at this very time, and contrary to all expectations, Israel's patrimony!

The undefiled army with which Providence has sent me hither, led by justice and accompanied by victory, has made Jerusalem my headquarters, and will, within a few days, transfer them to Damascus, a proximity which is no longer terrifying to David's city.

Rightful Heirs of Palestine!

The great nation which does not trade in men and countries as did those who sold your ancestors unto all peoples (Joel 4:6) hereby calls on you not indeed to conquer your patrimony, nay, only to take over that which has been conquered and, with that nation's warranty and support, to maintain it against all comers.

Arise! Show that the once overwhelming might of your oppressors has not repressed the courage of the des-

cendants of those heroes whose brotherly alliance did honor to Sparta and Rome (Macc. 12:15), but that all the two thousand years of slavish treatment have not succeeded in stifling it.

Hasten! Now is the moment which may not return for thousands of years, to claim the restoration of your rights among the population of the universe which had been shamefully withheld from you for thousands of years, your political existence as a nation among the nations, and the unlimited natural right to worship Yehovah in accordance with your faith, publicly and in likelihood for ever (Joel 4:20).

Nothing is known about the manner in which the Proclamation was actually issued. A pertinent passage in Napoleon's memoirs deals at some length with the practice of issuing proclamations and other messages to the populations of Palestine and the neighboring countries prior to the siege of Acre:

Berthier utilized this pause in order to despatch proclamations to Jerusalem, to Nazareth, to the Lebanon. These were proclamations of the Sultan el Kebir [i.e., Bonaparte] to the Turks, addresses from the priests of Gama el Azhar to the Moslem faithful, and finally circular letters to the Christians. These proclamations were in Arabic: headquarters had a printing press.[38]

Another source, the above-quoted letter of Bonaparte to General Régnier of March 9 indicates the number of the distributed copies: eight or ten copies were considered sufficient for the proclamation to the inhabitants of Jerusalem,

and various channels were used in order to secure the arrival
of at least one of the leaflets. An analogous method of distribution may be assumed for the manifesto to the Jewish Nation, and it is probable that the printing press had Hebrew
type in addition to the Latin, Greek, Arabic, and Syriac letters, the printing material having been provided from Rome
with the help of Vatican experts. If, however, Hebrew letters
were not available, handwriting would have served just as
well.

It is probable that the Proclamation or at least its first
draft was, in accordance with Bonaparte's habit, dictated by
him to a secretary. We may assume that Bonaparte, in draft-
ing addresses which required a translation into an Oriental
language, made use of the expert Orientalists who were at
his disposal. Although he obviously composed the documents
in French, their form and partly even their contents had to
be adapted to the special Oriental language and to the spirit
of the respective nation. The obvious candidate would have
been Venture de Paradis, Bonaparte's Orientalist, interpreter,
and faithful adviser.

Even so, it must be borne in mind that the Proclamation
was not of a merely local or regional character but destined
to reach the Jews in the various parts of the Diaspora. The
use of French alone or in addition to a Hebrew version must
therefore have been necessary. The issue of the Proclamation
in two languages would also accord with the practice which
Napoleon observed later on when he issued proclamations
destined for non-French territories: they were usually bilin-
gual, in the native tongue and in French.

A document, discovered simultaneously with the Procla-

mation, happens to be the translated text of a covering letter
of the Proclamation:

> *Aaron, son of Levi, Rabbi of Jerusalem, to the Chil-*
> *dren of Captivity in the lands of sunrise and of sunset,*
> *of noon and midnight!*

> *Jerusalem, in the month of Nissan in the year 5559*

> *Albeit there is no need to add anything to the letter*
> *which the man after the Lord's heart, Bonaparte, that*
> *great and high enlightened Commander-in-Chief of the*
> *French armies in Africa and Asia, has addressed to*
> *you, I, Aaron son of Levi, of the tribe of Levi, by the*
> *mercy of our God, the Lord Zabaoth, after the passing*
> *of innumerable generations again here, First Rabbi and*
> *Priest in this Holy City, have, for the sake of the weak,*
> *thought fit to remind them of the words of Joel son of*
> *Pethuel, Chapter 4, and of Zephaniah son of Cushi,*
> *Chapter 2, and Malachi, Chapter 2, 3.*

> *Brethren! The so glorious prophecies contained therein*
> *have been, as to their larger part, already fulfilled by*
> *the victorious army of the great nation, and it now de-*
> *pends only on us, to behave not as the children of har-*
> *lots and adulteresses, but as true descendants of Israel,*
> *and to desire the inheritance of the people of the Lord*
> *and the beautiful services of the Lord, Psalm of David*
> *27:4.*

> *Take then unto yourselves the wings of the eagle and*
> *the strength of the lioness, like unto our fathers in the*
> *days of Nehemiah, son of Hacaliah, and Ezra, son of*

Seraiah, to rebuild the walls of the orphaned city and temple to the Lord in which His Glory shall dwell from now for evermore.

Proclaim this to all nations among whom Jacob's seed is scattered, sanctify a combat, arouse the stronger, let all men of Israel, capable of bearing arms gather and come up to us, let even the weak say: I am strong! Joel 4.

May the God of Abraham, of Isaac and Jacob bless the work of our hands! May He do and accomplish this, as He has sworn to our fathers! May He remember for good all that the great nation has done unto us, Ezra 7:27, and let the whole people cry as of Gideon, son of Joash, Judges 7:

Here the Sword of the Lord and of Bonaparte!

The letter seems to have been written simultaneously with the Proclamation or immediately after its issue. The Hebrew date corroborates this assumption. The first day of that month of Nissan fell on April 6, 1799. The date of the Proclamation — April 20, 1799 — coincides therefore with the 15 of Nissan, the first day of Passover. The indication of Jerusalem as the place where the letter was written conforms with the Proclamation. All these circumstances suggest that the letter was more than a covering letter: It was a premeditated counterpart to Bonaparte's Proclamation to the Jewish nation. Its purpose was to serve both as an instrument of communication with the Diaspora and as a Jewish testimony to the genuineness of Bonaparte's manifesto.

9

THE AUTHORSHIP AND THE DATE OF THE
PROCLAMATION

The Proclamation is dated: "General Headquarters, Jerusalem." This is evidently incorrect; in fact, a bold misrepresentation of the real state of affairs. And yet the puzzling statement loses much of its mystery at closer inspection. It was, above all, neither the first nor the last premature date which Napoleon Bonaparte used in reports or proclamations. His regard for maximum effectiveness prompted him to take liberties in selecting the most proper date or place for his announcements. During the siege of Toulon he gave an account of the retreat of the British fleet, four hours before his guns were in a position to fire on it. As Emperor he took care that the *Moniteur* announced the Concordat before it had been concluded. He personally sent news which ostensibly came from Constantinople, and inserted in the *Moniteur* letters which he claimed had been written by subordinates.

Bonaparte's absolute certainty of the imminent fall of Acre made him anticipate, with equal certainty, the capture of Jerusalem. The capital had been at his mercy even before the siege of Acre. In any case, no opposition of the Jerusalem

garrison was to be expected after the battle at Mount Tabor,
and certainly not after a defeat or even capture of Jazzar
Pasha. There can hardly be any doubt that, whatever Bonaparte's real plans after the fall of Acre might have been,
the triumphal entry in Jerusalem, the "liberated Jerusalem,"
was an inevitable part of them.

Bonaparte's call was not to the Jewish inhabitants of Palestine who knew that Jerusalem remained in Turkish hands.
It was a call to *return* addressed to the dispersed Children
of Israel, the "exiled" dispersed nation, "the Rightful Heirs
of Palestine." Jerusalem was for them almost identical with
the Land of Israel. Owing to contemporary means of communication the Proclamation could not reach the important
Jewish centers until some time had elapsed. Bonaparte was
sure that by the time it did reach them, Jerusalem would be
his. Whoever claimed to have conquered the Land was supposed to be in Zion. From no other city was an offer of the
Land of Israel to the Jewish people as its rightful heritage
permitted.

10

CONTENTS, STYLE, AND ESSENCE OF THE PROCLAMATION

The Proclamation to the Jewish Nation offers striking analogies to some proclamations issued by Bonaparte in the same period. Justified as, for instance, the reference to the sufferings of the Jews was, this passage has counterparts in equally strong accusations against the oppressors of other nations. Moreover, here as there, the generosity of the French nation is contrasted with the tyranny of France's enemies. "The despot who so long has enslaved Lombardy has caused great mischief to France, but the French know that the cause of kings is not that of the people" — reads a passage in the proclamation to the people of Lombardy of May 19, 1796. The manifesto to the Egyptians, too, contains a similar and very elaborate antithesis. The conformities of the manifesto to the Jewish nation with many of Bonaparte's utterances, especially the similarity of the "emotional vocabulary," indicate to what great extent the Proclamation was an example of a general Napoleonic type.[89]

The offer of Palestine to the Jews of the world was categorical and unconditional. It was an official statement made by the French nation. In considering the seriousness of the offer, it is essential to bear in mind that it was made at a moment when Bonaparte regarded himself as the master of Palestine: he felt entitled to date the Proclamation from Jerusalem. The emphasis laid on the fact that the Jewish people need only take over, not conquer, Palestine corresponds both with the strategic situation, as Bonaparte saw it, and with the conception of Israel's right to its heritage.

The offer of the French nation had therefore, logically, to be addressed to the Jewish people as a whole, not to a special section of Jewry. In this respect the Proclamation corresponds with the *"Letter to the Brethren"* in which, without regard to frontiers, Jews all over the globe were invited to form a joint representative body for the purpose of negotiating with the Directory. Thus, the Proclamation was, in contrast to the other proclamations which were issued by Bonaparte during the Eastern campaign, not an appeal to the local population. It neither contained the usual appeal for submission, nor any threat to those who would not cooperate with the French. It was particularly not an appeal for military aid. The Proclamation declared that a military action was not needed because the conquest of Palestine was already an accomplished fact.

What purpose did Bonaparte pursue with the issue of the Proclamation? According to the notice of the *Moniteur*, the Proclamation was addressed to the Jews of Asia and Africa only, and the contents of the manifesto were described as an appeal to gather under the colors of Bonaparte in order to reestablish ancient Jerusalem; hence many historians were inclined to dismiss the Proclamation as a purely military measure. Thus, Heinrich Graetz declared that the Proclamation was intended to win Hayim Muallem Farḥi, Jazzar's loyal Jewish aide, for Bonaparte's cause, while Simon Dubnov considered it a trick aimed at the Jews of those countries. The growing understanding of the pre-Zionist movements led to a more correct appreciation of the Proclamation. Thus, Philip Guedalla, in his memorable lecture about *Napoleon and Palestine* (also a booklet), delivered before the Jewish Historical Society of England on May 25, 1935, arrived at the conclusion that Bonaparte "for a few weeks in the spring of 1799 was a momentary Zionist." Three years before the text was unearthed, Salo W. Baron summed up these views in a well-balanced resume:

> ...the famous proclamation of Napoleon to the Jewish people during the Egyptian campaign in 1799, although of little immediate consequence symbolized Europe's acknowledgment of Jewish rights to Palestine. Napoleon was no idealist, seeking to solve the Jewish question on an altruistic basis; his shrewd recognition of the intense interest of the Jews, whom he attempted to enlist in his expeditionary army, and of the support the Jewish hope had received from French and English writers, is a barometer of the extent to which the European atmosphere was charged with these messianic expections.[30]

On the other hand, a contemporary historian, Barbara W. Tuchman, despite full knowledge of the discovered wording of the Proclamation, stamped it as "a meaningless gesture, as artificial as any heroic strutting on the stage."[31]

The Proclamation was an instrument designed to influence

the Jews in favor of Revolutionary France and its victorious
General-in-Chief. Even more obviously, the offer of Palestine,
the flattering praise of the Jewish nation, and the sweeping
promises to her have the same objective. Bonaparte was
aware of the prominent position which some sectors of Western and Oriental Jewry held in finance and commerce. The
"Letter to the Brethren" and the corresponding article of
La Décade contained statements about the "immense riches"
of the Jews and expressed the hope that their owners would
use them in the interest of the Restoration of the Jewish
people. The prospect of linking the financial and commercial
forces of the Jews with the outcome, and possibly with the
extension, of the Eastern Expedition, could seem an enticing
goal to Bonaparte. The genesis of the Proclamation itself,
its unquestionable link with contemporary documents of the
Movement for the Restoration of the Jews, its antecedents
in previous public statements of Bonaparte, the roots which
the idea of Israel's revival had in Bonaparte's romanticism
and in his aspiration to create a national revolution in the
eastern Mediterranean and Asia, and finally the victorious
battle at Mount Tabor, with its prospect of Acre's seemingly
inevitable fall — all these aspects justify the Proclamation
on its own merits.

In the *Mémorial de St. Hélène* by Las Casas, Napoleon
is quoted:

> One of my grandest ideas was *l'agglomération*: the
> concentration of people geographically united, but sep-
> arated by revolutions and political action. There are,
> scattered over Europe, 30 million Frenchmen, 15 mil-

lion Spaniards, 15 million Italians, and 30 million Germans. My intention was to make each of these peoples into a separate national state [corps de nation].[32]

The application of this statement to the Proclamation is obvious. Bonaparte must have been inspired by the idea of uniting a nation which was scattered all over the globe! The issue of the Proclamation should thus be regarded as the climax of the Eastern Expedition.

11

THE ENIGMA: AARON SON OF LEVI, RABBI OF JERUSALEM

Among the many problems with which Bonaparte's experiment to restore the Jewish nation confronts us, none offers greater difficulties than the question, Who was the mysterious man who was chosen to transmit the offer of the French nation to the Diaspora: Aaron, son of Levi? There is no doubt that he was *not* the Chief Rabbi of Jerusalem nor his deputy. As external evidence is lacking, we must deduce his identity from the meager facts supplied by the text. There are good grounds for assuming that the writer of the covering letter was a newcomer to Palestine. He himself seems to suggest this by his astonishing claim to be "after the passing of innumerable generations, again here, in the Holy City, First Rabbi and Priest." This passage is apparently an allusion to "Ezra, the priest" (Ezra 7:11), whose book is twice mentioned in the *"Letter."* Moreover, the very address of the letter "to the Children of Captivity" is a quotation from Ezra 10:7, and the letter itself is conceived in the spirit of Ezra and Nehemia. All this can be taken as an indication that the writer of the letter pretended to be another Ezra or Nehemia who had been sent to Judah and Jerusalem

(Ezra 7: 14, Nehemiah 2: 4—6) to assist Bonaparte in the restoration of the Jewish nation.

If the hypothesis that the writer of the covering letter was a newcomer to Palestine, like the ancient leaders, is taken as a starting point for a further inquiry, the genuineness of the name "Aaron son of Levi" appears very doubtful. The confidential and dangerous character of the task of covering the offer of the French nation was certainly one of the reasons for concealing the authorship of the covering letter. On the other hand, "Aaron," the First High Priest, seemed a very appropriate name for a religious leader who claimed to be another Ezra or Nehemiah. Messianic pretenders often claimed a noble and sacred origin. The emphasis laid by the writer of the *"Letter"* on his descent from "the tribe of Levi" was well calculated; the restoration of Israel was indissolubly linked with the rebuilding of the Temple and with the revival of the ancient service, as well as of the office of the High Priest, who necessarily would have to be, like Aaron, a descendant of Levi. In fact, the chapters of Malachi which are referred to in the *"Letter"* contain passages dealing with "the covenant of Levi" (Malachi 3: 3).

"Aaron son of Levi" was a fictitious name which the writer of the covering letter chose in order to justify his claim to the dignity of "the Priest." The identity of the writer of the covering letter remains an open question. The author of the letter to the "Children of Captivity" might have been linked with the group of Italian Jews who had welcomed Bonaparte with exalted hopes as *ḥelek tov* "Good Portion" = Bona-Parte and *ohev Israel* "Lover of Israel", or even with the circles from which the *"Letter to the Brethren"* originated. The covering letter shows some features which are reminiscent of the *"Letter to the Brethren."* An identification of Rabbi Aaron with an Egyptian Jew is even more probable because Egyptian Jews joined the expeditionary corps and, above all, with regard to the appointment of two members of the Cairo community as *grands prêtres de la nation juive.* It would also fit the historical situation and Bonaparte's inclination to find analogies between his army and the Children of Israel who, coming from Egypt, invaded ancient Canaan. Thus the possibility remains that one of the newly created "High Priests" accompanied Bonaparte to Palestine and finally made the bold step of usurping the title of "First Rabbi and Priest in this Holy City." In fact, the phrase used in this connection in the covering letter, "after innumerable generations again here," would very well fit the claim of being a successor of Aaron, the first High Priest, who like Moses had been born in and came out from Egypt.

On the whole, an image of a faithful, zealous, indeed over-zealous, Jew, emerges from the "Letter." While the Proclamation deals with the historical, political, and legal aspects of the Restoration, Aaron ben Levi, confines himself to appealing to the religious feelings of the Jews and to rousing their hopes for the rebuilding of Jerusalem of the Temple. In conformity with the Proclamation, he declares that the prophecies have been, in their larger part, already fulfilled. But while the Proclamation refers, apart from Isaiah, only to Joel, the biblical references of the covering letter are far more numerous. It is particularly noteworthy that Zephaniah 2: 4 points to the strategic situation. This passage predicts not only the desolation of Gaza, Ashkelon, and

Ashdod, but also deals with Ekron which "shall be rooted up" — an illusion to the imminent capture of Acre.

"The powerful impact made by the battle at Mount Tabor on the native population was recorded by Napoleon in his memoirs: "The battle at Mount Tabor had the effect which it had promised: The Druse, the Maronites, the Christian population of Syria, and a few weeks later deputies from Armenia flocked to the French camp." Although Napoleon is silent about the Jews, he mentions them in another passage of the same chapter dealing with the siege of Acre which follows his remark about the expectations of the Jews. "Christian, Jewish, Moslem agents were dispatched to Damascus, Aleppo, and even to Armenia. They reported that the presence of the army in Syria agitated the minds of all the peoples."[33]

Thus, the feelings expressed in the covering letter were not confined to the writer alone. Rumors of the Proclamation — before and after its issue — might also have had their share in fostering the hope of the Jews in their impending deliverance through the strong arm of Bonaparte.

12

THE REPORT OF THE M O N I T E U R ABOUT
BONAPARTE'S PROCLAMATION

On May 22, 1799, the organ of the French Government, *Gazette Nationale ou le Moniteur Universel,* published a notice which read:

> (No. 243. Tridi, 3rd Prairial, year VII of the French Republic one and indivisible.)
>
> [Page] 389. Politics. Turkey, Constantinople, 28th Germinal [*i.e.,* April 17, 1799].
>
> Bonaparte caused to publish a proclamation, in which he invites all the Jews of Asia and Africa to come and range themselves under his banners in order to reestablish ancient Jerusalem.
>
> A great number of them have armed themselves already, and their battalions threaten Aleppo.
>
> The inhabitants in the environment of Damascus are in revolt against the Porte. The Grand Signior must leave for Syria in order to take personal command against Bonaparte. The Grand Vizier, too, must go abroad at the head of a considerable corps of the Janissaries.

The same notice was also published on the same day in the *Gazette de France.* The offer made by Bonaparte according to the *Moniteur* is formulated in the terms of the covering letter rather than of the Proclamation itself: the promise being the reestablishment of Jerusalem instead of the turning over of Palestine to the Jewish nation. The appeal to the Jews to range themselves under Bonaparte's banners corresponds with Rabbi Aaron's call to arms, but omits a reference to the already conquered land which has to be taken over by the Jews without fighting. Moreover, the Proclamation, as quoted in the *Moniteur,* was addressed to the Jews of Asia and Africa only and not to the whole Jewish nation in all countries of the Diaspora. Finally the date of the report from Constantinople — April 17, 1799 — though in accord with the circumstance that the Proclamation was issued only during the last stage of the Syrian campaign, precedes that of the Proclamation by three days.

This combination of consistency and contradiction loses much of its intricacy if viewed in the light of the specific historical situation. Philip Guedalla expressed the opinion that the report dated from Constantinople was based on a direct instruction from Bonaparte. Many circumstances justify this assumption. It is striking that no source of the Constantinople report is given. The news is based neither on a letter of an informant nor on the report of a courier, as was the rule with similar announcements. Moreover, the report appears as a rather well-calculated official statement. Such a statement was bound to differ from the proper Proclamation, which was secretly forwarded to the Diaspora by means of a Hebrew covering letter.

Compared with the text of the Proclamation, the notice
of the *Moniteur* presents the Restoration of the Jewish nation
as a more moderate undertaking. The appeal is addressed
to the Jews of Asia and Africa; the offer of Palestine is replaced by the prospect of reestablishing ancient Jerusalem;
the invitation to take over the legitimate inheritance is sub-
stituted by a call to rally under Bonaparte's banners. The
statement that Jewish "battalions" threatened Aleppo was
preceded and followed by similar reports in the French press.
The *Gazette de France* of 25 Floréal, Year VII (May 14,
1799) reported from Constantinople under 21 Germinal
(April 10) that a courier had arrived with five very alarming
dispatches. According to one of them, Bonaparte had detached General Kléber with an army of Copts, Greeks, and
Jews, supported by a French corps of 5000 men. On 8 Prairial, Year VII (May 27, 1799), only five days after the appearance of the report about Bonaparte's Proclamation, the
Moniteur published a report from Zemun under 9 Floréal
(29 April) — *i.e.,* eight days after the issue of the Proclamation — according to which a revolutionary movement was
in progress in Greece owing to the rumor that Bonaparte
was about to march against Constantinople with an army
composed of French, Copts, Greeks, Jews, Armenians, etc.
The notice in the *Moniteur* of May 22 was, however, the first
and only one in which the participation of Jews in the Syrian
campaign was mentioned without a simultaneous reference
to Copts, Greeks, or other native populations.

The report of the Proclamation could have reached Constantinople either by sea or by land. We know from Bonaparte's correspondence that he made several attempts to

communicate with Constantinople by sea. Communications with Turkey were, however, also maintained through runners by land. It is, nevertheless, doubtful whether Bonaparte actually dispatched the report to the French agent in Constantinople with the instruction to forward it to Paris and whether the news about the issue of the Proclamation reached the Western world via Constantinople. Turkey was at the time at war with France. The chances of getting news by this route safely to France were not favorable. It is reasonable to assume that the report, with a fictitious date from Constantinople, was sent — presumably by land — directly to France. Such a procedure was in accordance with a frequently repeated Napoleonic practice. Emperor Napoleon Bonaparte had a predilection for Constantinople as a fictitious source of political news.[34] The date of the report, under the plausible assumption that Constantinople was in this case merely an imaginary place name, loses its problematic character. The seventeenth of April was the day after the battle at Mount Tabor. The Proclamation might have been, as pointed out above, composed on that day. The date was therefore either correct or — as in a message whose origin had to be concealed — arbitrarily chosen.

When the news about Bonaparte's manifesto arrived in Paris, about one year had passed since *La Décade* had published the article in which the Restoration of Israel had been advocated so forcefully. Now *La Décade* was again ready to comment on what seemed to be a fulfillment of that prediction. The writer of an article published on 10 Prairial, Year VII (May 29, 1799), No. 25, may have had at his disposal a different, more specific, report. He not only re-

ferred to the Proclamation as proclaiming "the deliverance
of Jerusalem and Judaea," but expressly added: Bonaparte
"appealed in their [the Jews'] ancient fatherland to the Jews
dispersed over the globe." Thus, at variance with the report
of the *Moniteur* and in accordance with the actual Proclamation, not only the Jews of Asia and Africa, but those of the
whole Diaspora were denoted as addressees of the Proclamation. In consequence the writer commented rather exuber-
antly:

> "Who knows? They will perhaps see in him [Bonaparte]
> the Messiah, and soon twenty prophecies will have pre-
> dicted the event, the epoch, and even the circumstances
> of his coming. It is at least very probable that the Jewish
> people is about to transform itself again into a national
> body, that the Temple of Solomon will be rebuilt..."

PART FOUR

THE FATE AND ECHO OF THE PROCLAMATION

13

BONAPARTE'S RETREAT FROM THE HOLY LAND AND THE DISAPPEARANCE OF THE PROCLAMATION

On April 24, Napoleon ordered a general assault on Acre. The walls of the fortress did not yield to the heavy guns in which he had put great confidence, and the bravery of his men again dashed itself against British tenacity and Mohammedan fanaticism. April 25 saw a repetition of the bombardment and of the attack. Four further assaults, on May 1, 7, 8 and 10, though equally futile, testify to the desperate persistence with which he stuck to his goal. Eight generals lost their lives near Acre. Perhaps Bonaparte might have continued his attempts if mightier forces had not interfered. The plague reappeared and claimed nearly 3,000 men. On May 10, Bonaparte addressed a report of the Syrian campaign to the Directory. The document concluded with the evasive passage: "The season is too far advanced; the aim which I had set myself is accomplished; Egypt is calling me." A week later, on May 17, he issued a proclamation in which he announced the end of the siege. On May 20, Bonaparte raised the siege of Acre, covering the evacuation by a heavy cannonade. The retreat from Syria began. Among the dead left behind was Venture de Paradis. Venture's death was an inestimable loss for the history of the Oriental Expedition and particularly of the Syrian campaign. It meant that the memoirs of the man who participated in the most intimate way in Bonaparte's dealings with the population of Egypt and Palestine were to remain unwritten. Thus, Venture took with him into his grave the secret of the circumstances under which the Proclamation was created and issued.

In view of the retreat from the Land of Israel, the appeal to the Jews, urging them to "take over that which has been conquered," became a mockery.

The date and text of the manifesto contained statements which never materialized. Bonaparte must have been most anxious to obliterate so compromising a document. But whereas he was unable to repeal the *Moniteur,* the suppression of the Proclamation itself was possible. In all probability very few copies of the Proclamation were sent out before the expected entry into Jerusalem. There was no difficulty in stopping their distribution or in recalling the few sheets which had already been sent out.

In his efforts to erase the memory of the Proclamation, Bonaparte was undoubtedly supported by the Jews themselves. Those loyal to the Turkish government certainly opposed any attempt to disseminate copies of the manifesto. Besides, the retreat of the French created a catastrophic situation for the Jews of Palestine. According to the traveler John Lewis Burckhardt, the Jewish quarter of Safed was completely sacked after the return of the Turks from Acre. Copies of the Proclamation still found in Palestine at that time hardly had a chance to survive.

Under these circumstances, Bonaparte could feel justified in assuming that he had wiped out the vestiges of his Proclamation to the Rightful Heirs of Palestine. In fact, if there would have been no notice in the *Moniteur,* the issue of the Proclamation would have remained entirely hidden from the world. It was by this isolated news item that the story of the Proclamation became known and Napoleon preferred ignoring it altogether. Absolute silence about the episode seemed to be a sufficient means of effacing the memory of the Proclamation; by the same method Trafalgar was to be "rubbed out of existence."

In a quite different manner Bonaparte dealt with the disastrous last phase of the campaign. In the bulletin he issued on June 14, before his entry into Cairo, the ramparts of Acre and Jazzar's palace were described as a heap of ruins and Jazzar himself as seriously wounded. The captured prisoners and bags were mentioned with pride as witnesses of a victory. In fact, the idea of another campaign toward the East was born in Bonaparte's mind almost at the very moment of his arrival at Cairo. He wrote to the Directory on June 28 that if they could send 15,000 more men, "We shall be able to go everywhere, even to Constantinople."

In Paris the expectations which had accompanied the publication of the Proclamation soon calmed down. An article signed "David" dealing with "the probable conquest of the Ottoman empire by Bonaparte" was published in the *Moniteur* of 9 Messidor (July 27, 1799). It contained the strange passage:

> Let us await the confirmation of this happy news. If it is premature, we would like to think that some day it will be realized. It is not only in order to give Jerusalem back to the Jews that Bonaparte has conquered Syria.

In the meantime Bonaparte, in a brilliant action, had defeated the Turkish expeditionary corps at Aboukir Bay (July 25). It was his last military feat on Egyptian soil. He had warded off invasions from land and sea and made himself free for the return to France. Alarming news reached him from Europe. The French armies had been defeated in Italy and on the Rhine. All his achievements and all the territorial acquisitions of the Republic were in jeopardy. His homecoming was a dire necessity and a great new opportunity. He entrusted General Kléber with the command of the army of occupation and left Egypt on August 23.

Thus, the year 1799 which had seen Bonaparte before the walls of Acre and retreating from them saw him, six months later, taking the first step toward the imperial throne. Bonaparte remained intent on suppressing the memory of the document that instead of signalizing the liberation of Jerusalem had become a testimony to his first and most ominous defeat. The frustrated attempt to restore the Jewish people to Palestine became taboo to Napoleon. Bonaparte, nevertheless, could not help alluding to the move he had made before Acre in favor of the revival of the Jewish nation. At a meeting of the State Council on the occasion of a debate on colonial affairs, on August 16, 1800, he declared:

> It was by becoming a Catholic that I ended the Vendée war. It was by becoming a Musulman that I established myself in Egypt, by becoming an Ultramontane that I gained the priests of Italy. If I governed a nation of Jews I should reestablish the Temple of Solomon.[35]

It is easy to brand this dictum as the expression of unscrupulous opportunism. But foolish as it would be to deny its opportunist quality, there is no justification for disregarding the equally inherent element of toleration. It was this philosophical principle which led Napoleon to the conclusion that the ruler has to identify himself with the religious beliefs of the governed people. The Proclamation bears evidence that in relation to the Jewish people such an identification was not a hypothetical possibility but a fact.

14

VOICES FROM ENGLAND

In no part of the world was Bonaparte's Expedition to the East watched with closer attention than in Great Britain. The impending transformation of the Holy Land's destiny provoked lively interest, particularly among adherents of the movement for the Restoration of the Jews. Extraordinary publicity was given to the *"Letter to the Brethren,"* and an animated literary discussion began about the chances of a speedy Restoration of the Jews with reference to the supposed aims of the French Expedition to the Orient.

Edward King, author of *Remarks on the Signs of the Times* (1798), interpreted the happenings in France and in the Near East as a fulfillment of the prophecy in Isaiah 18, concluding that the Restoration of the Jews was impending. Samuel Horsley, Lord Bishop of Rochester, replied at length to King in his *Critical Disquisitions on the Eighteenth Chapter of Isaiah, in a Letter to Edward King, Esq., F.E.A.S.* (1799). The Bishop subjected King's arguments to an extensive theological examination, and, while rejecting his conclusions, did not deny the possibility of a "partial" restoration.

History, the Interpreter of Prophecy (1799) by Henry Kett,

a fellow of Trinity College, Oxford, contained a clear distinction between the bodily return of the Jews and the religious
implications of the event. The following passage reads, indeed, like a direct allusion to the Proclamation:

> It cannot be imagined that the Jews would see with in-
> difference the fall of the Turkish empire, which has so
> long "trodden down Jerusalem": their hope of deliver-
> ance would be naturally raised to a height unknown
> for many ages; and their prophecies would be examined
> with redoubled attention. A general council... may be
> called, or at least measures taken for a general consulta-
> tion. And this dispersed neglected people may become,
> at an awful period, of inexpressible importance in the
> political, as well as in the religious world. It certainly
> is not impossible that the French *may offer them the
> ancient land* [italics are mine] with the double view of
> contradicting the word of Prophecy, and of attaching a
> powerful people, whom they affect to call Republicans,
> to their interest; in order to render them subservient to
> their designs of universal conquest (Vol. II p. 301–2).

Nevertheless, Kett thought it unlikely that France would complete the task of restoring the Jewish people. "The reestablishment of the Jews in their own land by Bonaparte," Kett
argues, "would rouse the world in arms against it." He was
one of the first writers of that period to suggest that Britain
might be the power chosen to fulfill the Restoration prophecy. "Is it an improbable conjecture," he asked, "...that
this maritime, commercial, protestant kingdom should take
the lead in executing the Divine will on such an occasion?"

The hope for Israel's immediate restoration was raised in France as well by an Irish Protestant from County Cork, Thomas Corbet, a graduate of Trinity College, Dublin. He was a brother of General William Corbet, one of the "United Irishmen" who fought for Ireland and against England by joining France's armies. On February 17, 1799, he addressed a letter to Barras, the predominant member of the Directory, suggesting the creation of an autonomous Jewish colony near the Isthmus and the Red Sea; the Jews of the Diaspora should provide the sum needed for purchasing the land. Under French tutelage the Jews would become good warriors and push further ahead and reestablish their republic. Corbet confessed that the plan was inspired by the activities of Napoleon in Egypt.

The decisive step made by Bonaparte toward Israel's Restoration and the far-reaching political implications of this move were clearly realized by the Anabaptist James Bicheno who, in his book, *The Restoration of the Jews: The Crisis of All Nations* (1800), presented the Restoration of the Jews as one of the world-pressing problems. Bonaparte appeared to him not as the Antichrist or as the representative of an anti-Christian power, but as an instrument, albeit unconscious and reluctant, of Divine will. "I freely acknowledge," Bicheno declared, "that from the footing which the French had got in the Turkish empire, near to the Promised Land, — if not in it... — I cannot help feeling that we are not the favored nation."

A reply by Thomas Witherby, *Observations on Mr. Bicheno's Book Entitled "Restoration of the Jews: The Crisis of All Nations,"* rejected any alliance with a Power "which had turned away from God," *i.e.*, with the Republic of France. Only an inner transformation of the Jewish nation and the fulfillment of the tasks assigned to her by Providence would, through the medium of a Christian Power, bring about the Restoration. In a second work, *Attempt to Remove Prejudices Concerning the Jewish Nation,* published three years later, Witherby firmly defended his conviction that "no atheistical democracy, no revolutionary government, but a pious sovereign, great in power and greater in piety and virtue, beloved by his subjects as their father, was to become the new Cyrus for the Jewish Nation."

15

THE REACTION OF THE DIASPORA

In contrast to the well-documented, open, and forceful reaction which was evoked in English gentile quarters by the
invasion of the Holy Land, the attitude of the English Jews
is shrouded in darkness. To be sure, an astonishing passage
regarding this question is to be found in the "Letters from
England," published under the pseudonym Don Manuel
Alvares Espriella, in 1807, by the Poet Laureate, Robert
Southey:

> It may well be supposed that when Bonaparte was in
> Syria his movements were anxiously watched by the
> Jews. There was a great stir among them, and it is prob-
> able that if he had invited them by proclamation, and
> promised to give them Palestine, armies would have
> been raised to take and keep possession of that Holy
> Land, to which they look individually and collectively,
> as their gathering place.[38]

The statement about the behavior of the Jews seems to be
based on personal experience. No other proof has come down
to us concerning an active interest of the English Jews in
Bonaparte's revivalist plans. Only few years had passed since

Jews had been suspected of Jacobinic sympathies, and anti-Jewish riots had had to be suppressed at Ipswich. The Alien Act of 1793, too, spelled the danger of deportation for many Jews.

There is, however, a telling testimony to an opposite trend among contemporary British Jewry. David Levi, a learned hat-maker who enjoyed considerable literary reputation, published, between 1796 and 1800, a three-volume work entitled *Dissertations on the Prophecies of the Old Testament, Containing All Such Prophecies as Are Applicable to the Coming of the Messiah; the Restoration of the Jews and the Resurrection of the Dead; Whether so Applied by Jews or Christians.* In this work Levi sought to bring out the differences between the Jewish and Christian doctrines of Restoration. He maintained that the Jewish people would fulfill its mission of redemption while being scattered rather than by returning to its homeland and refused to indulge in any speculation concerning the date of the Messianic age. Like the exodus from Egypt, the Restoration, he felt, would be the work of God alone.

In Germany the notice about the Proclamation had appeared in the widely read liberal *Vossische Zeitung,* which counted among its contributors writers like the champion of the Jewish cause, G. E. Lessing, and could not have escaped the attention of educated German Jews. Nothing, however, seems to have been more remote from the sphere of their interests than this appeal. David Friedländer, friend and pupil of Moses Mendelssohn, the militant pioneer of Enlightenment, and leader of the Jews in Prussia, addressed an anonymous Epistle on behalf "of several heads of families of the Jewish religion" to the head of the Protestant Consistory in Berlin, Pastor Teller. The letter pleaded for a compromise between Judaism and Christianity. The elders claimed to be ready to subscribe to Christian tenets as far as these were not contrary to reason, as was the belief that Jesus was the Son of God. They made no objection to Baptism, as a symbol of solidarity with the Church; the Jewish community was thus supposed to become a sect within Protestantism.

The proposition was preceded by a sharp denunciation of Jewish ceremonial law and of the Messianic idea. The utter rejection of the latter and of all national aspirations was one of the main concerns of the authors. He dwelt upon it in great length:

> Sad and depressed we face the history of the Jews who have ceased to be called and to be a nation... The people, dispersed in the whole world, without a lasting dwelling place... without a civic head, without a spiritual leader, left to itself, has lost the feeling for the value of reason and the understanding of the higher truths... On top of all this, the idea of a Messiah was added which has totally confused the heads and has prevented them from a free judgement... This expectation of the Messiah and of the return to the Promised Land has necessarily strengthened the inclination to concentrate all the diligence and contemplation on the ancient history, on the service in the Temple, on the sacrifices and the ceremonial law. The prayers which they composed resounded of endlessly repeated laments

over the lost land... In all these prayers without excep-
tion... the lamenting cries of slaves who long for redemption and the prayer for a Messiah was heard who
would lead the dispersed remnants of Israel back to
Palestine.

The utterly negative attitude toward the restoration of the
Jewish people, as expressed in the letter, became the keynote
of the Reform movement which soon was to play an important role in Jewish religious life in Germany.

The situation in the northern provinces of the Austrian
empire, Bohemia, and Moravia, with their ancient and well-
established Jewish communities of Prague, Nikolsburg, and
other cities, seems, at first glance, to conform to the general
pattern of indifference and disregard. And yet, in *this* part of
the Austrian Empire Bonaparte's Proclamation reached the
representatives of the Jewish people, and was acclaimed by
them. Moreover, there is not only documentary evidence
available about their positive reaction to the Proclamation,
but it is just this isolated incident in the history of the Proclamation which finally led to the preservation of the text of
Bonaparte's manifesto.

16

THE FRANKISTS OF BOHEMIA HAIL THE PROCLAMATION AND STIR THE COMMU- NITY OF PRAGUE

Situated in the middle of Europe, the Jewry of Bohemia and Moravia formed a major center of the Diaspora. Rabbi Judah Löw ben Bezalel of Prague, the celebrated "High Rabbi," gathered around him at the turn of the sixteenth and seventeenth centuries a circle of scholars versed in the Talmud and interested in science and philosophy as well. While legend has credited him with the making and the eventual destruction of the Golem, history testifies that he advanced education on almost modern lines. On the other hand, one of the Rabbi's principal works, *Nezah Israel,* a mystical apology for Judaism, was permeated with Messianic ideas; thus Rabbi Löw became the very embodiment of the spirit which distinguished the best exponents of Bohemian and Moravian Jewry down the centuries by its peculiar blend of realism and mysticism.

The soil of Bohemia and Moravia proved particularly susceptible to the belief in Sabbatai Zevi, the false Messiah, at a time when the whole Jewish world was seized by a feverish expectation of his triumphant entry into Constantinople. In Moravia, disturbances among the Jews became so serious that the authorities had been obliged to issue public orders to calm the people. The Bohemian and Moravian communities remained in the forefront of the Sabbatean movement after the catastrophe and the subsequent death of its hero. When Nehemiah Ḥiyya Ḥayon, an eccentric cabbalist, who developed the trinitarian doctrine of the three divine persons (Parẓufim) — the holy primeval god, the holy father, and the *Shekhinah* (Divine Presence), the female person — arrived in 1711 in Prague, his ideas gained great popularity; during his stay (to 1712) Sabbateanism took new roots among Bohemian Jewry. Thus, a considerable Sabbatean group came into being in Prague in the first quarter of the eighteenth century. Rabbi Naphtali ben Isaac Katz (ha-Kohen), a great-grandson of the Great Rabbi Löw, one of the greatest rabbinical authorities of his time, was an adherent of cabbalistic magic and settled at that time in Prague and increased the fame of Prague as a center of the Cabbala. Nevertheless, the majority of the community rejected the mystical trend and staged a vigorous campaign against the heretics, which culminated in their anathematization on September 16, 1726. Among the rabbis who signed the great ban was Rabbi Jonathan E. Bybeschuetz, an outstanding talmudist, who was subsequently suspected of being a sympathizer, if not a member of the sect. Jacob Emden, an eminent scholar of Altona, accused him of having referred, in cabbalistic amulets, to Sabbatai Zevi.

One hundred years after the birth of Sabbatai Zevi, in 1726, in the Podolian city of Korolowka, the last of the Messianic pretenders, Jacob ben Judah Leibowicz, known as Jacob Frank, was born. He was a younger contemporary of Israel ben Eliezer Shem-Tov — the Baalshem Tov — the founder of the Ḥasidic movement, whose birthplace was not far away. Both mystics were deeply steeped in the Cabbala and contributed to the opposition to rigid Orthodoxy and to the yearning for revival among the Jewish masses of Poland. Jacob Frank was exposed in his youth to strong Sabbataean influences by his father. Forced to emigrate by the Orthodox rabbis, the Leibowicz family settled in Wallachia. Jacob, after having married Hana, the daughter of a native merchant, in 1753 in Nikopol, proceeded to Turkey where he visited Constantinople and Smyrna, Sabbatai Zevi's birthplace, and finally settled in Salonika. There he joined the Sabbatean Dönmeh sect and succeeded in becoming their leader. Upon his return to Podolia, Frank was acclaimed by the Sabbateans of his homeland who considered him to be the reincarnation of Sabbatai Zevi. His doctrine, as expounded in the *Book of the Words of the Lord*, has been called, by Gershom Sholem, "perhaps the most remarkable 'holy writ' which has ever been produced." It amounts, in the words of the same author, to a "veritable religious myth of nihilism" being the "conception of voluntary Marranism with the slogan: 'We must *all* descend into the realm of evil in order to vanquish it from within.'"[37]

Frank preached — and carried out — antinomian doctrines and conducted disputations with rabbis in Lvov under the auspices of the Catholic Church whose favor he tried to obtain. In the course of the disputations Frank repudiated the Talmud and lent his disreputable authority to blood libel canards. He eventually accepted baptism with many of his followers; King Augustus III of Poland and Saxony was his godfather. His patron bishop died shortly thereafter and

Frank was accused of heresy and imprisoned for thirteen years.

In 1773, Jacob Frank, accompanied by members of his family and eighteen attendants arrived in Brno (Brünn), the Moravian capital. A continuous flow of subsidies from his followers in Poland and other countries enabled Frank to establish a princely household there. His entourage increased after a while to several hundred persons, mostly young men and beautiful women. His rides through the city and to church resembled, by their splendor, processions of sovereign rulers. Frank intended to pierce the outer and inner walls of the ghetto and to establish a new community of Jews bound together by the revolt against rigid Orthodoxy.

To be sure, a stern opposition was put up against Frank and the Frankists — the *Maaminim* ("Believers"), as they called themselves — by Orthodox Jews and their rabbis. An attempt was made to obtain an official banishment of the Frankists from the capital, but the Austrian magistrates turned it down. It was said that Maria Theresa favored his stay, hoping that he would help bring the Jews into the fold of the Catholic Church. Nevertheless, the uneasiness caused by the enmity of the major part of the Jewish population induced Frank to leave Moravia in 1786.

The city of Offenbach near Frankfurt on the Main, in the Grand Duchy of Hesse, became the new residence of the Frankists. The financial means put at Frank's disposal by his admirers enabled him to acquire from the Prince of Isenburg the spacious castle of Offenbach with all the rights of sovereignty. The castle offered comfortable lodging for Frank's family, his entire newly installed court, and his followers, whose number amounted finally to about 1,000 souls. The settlement was called *Mahaneh* ("Camp") and the young men of the Frankist community were trained and organized on military lines. Dressed in a special red uniform and armed with rifles, they guarded the castle and served as Frank's bodyguard. One of their particular duties was to escort Frank and his family on their weekly church-going trips. A selected group of youth, the *Liberia,* was entrusted with attending on Frank himself and his confidents, the *Malkhut* ("the Government"). The pageantry of the Offenbach Court was a clear expression of Frank's determination to maintain and develop the framework of an independent and sovereign Jewish community.

In Bohemia, Frankists were a rather small group; about fifty persons in Prague and in two other communities of northern Bohemia, Kolin and Jicin, were members of the sect. Although they believed in the divine mission of Jacob Frank their faith was deeply rooted in the morally and intellectually distinctive tradition of Prague. It was, above all, a matter of principle among them to remain within the Jewish fold. They not only rejected conversion to Christianity, but attended the synagogues and painstakingly fulfilled their social duties toward the community. To be sure, their Judaism was permeated by cabbalistic views; the Messianic hope was for them no vague, distant prospect, but a definite expectation of a national and universal redemption. In fact, they firmly believed that salvation was near at hand and indulged in computations of the date of the Messianic kingdom. Since the rise of Bohemian Frankism coincided with the political upheaval in the Western world, its Messianic

element was nourished by the exciting course of contemporary events. The peculiar character of the Bohemian Frankists
manifested itself in their recognized leader, Jonas Beer Wehle.
This distinguished merchant of Prague, the offspring of an
old and celebrated family, was at the same time an original
thinker, whose particular pantheon had room for Moses
Mendelssohn and Immanuel Kant side by side with Sabbatai
Zevi and Isaac Luria. Wehle's house was the center of the
Bohemian Frankists. There they gathered almost daily for
common readings of the *Zohar* and other religious writings.

The emergence within the Bohemian community of a
Frankist group provoked sharp opposition in Orthodox
quarters. The first rebuke came from Rabbi Ezekiel Landau,
Chief Rabbi of Prague (1720–1793) who succeeded in
causing the Frankists to restrict their journeys to Brno and
Offenbach. His successor was Rabbi Eleazar Fleckeles
(1754–1826), a descendant of the Great Rabbi Löw, a distinguished scholar and preacher, well-known throughout the
whole Diaspora. On the first of the Penitential *Selihot* Days
before the New Year 5559, he ascended the pulpit of the
Venerable "Altneuschul" synagogue in order to deliver his
first sermon against the Frankists (1798). The rabbi warned
the community against intercourse with any person suspected
of being a Sabbataean. In an obvious allusion to Jonas Beer
Wehle, Fleckeles denoted the main features of a devout
Frankist as a predilection for the *Aggadot* and the *Zohar*
and for computating the coming of the Messiah. He casti-
gated those sending their children to Offenbach and added
sarcastically: "Are there too few military people and stra-
tegists among the kings and princes of this country? And

for what purposes are not only men, but also women and
children running to that place?" The sectarians were deceived
deceivers, misled people who pursued a chimera, whose belief in a Messiah — the false Messiah Jacob Frank — was
nothing else than a repetition of the Sabbatean heresy. Rabbi
Fleckeles did not realize that this explanation covered only
one half of the truth. What he ignored and, in fact, was unable to understand was the driving force behind the continuous flight of a minority from the ghetto of Prague to
the messianic military camp of Offenbach: the yearning for
an instant spiritual and moral revival, the expectation of a
new order of things, the desire to join the revolutionary
forces which were on the move outside the Jewish world.
The hurricane which swept the Western world had penetrated the walls of the ghetto of Prague and had made many
thirsty for fresh, invigorating air. These students of the Cabbala had been influenced by Jean-Jacques Rousseau, as well
as by German, French, and English classical and Romantic
writers. There was, for some Jewish children of that epoch,
no more romantic place in the world than the fabulous castle
of Offenbach.

Above all, this was the year 1798. Nine years had passed
since the storming of the Bastille, and the decree which se-
cured equal rights to the Jews of France had changed the
map of Europe. The fame of General Bonaparte, the *helek
tov,* had reached the ghetto of Prague; when the news arrived
that his army had entered Papal Rome and crushed the
power of *Edom,* the cabbalist circle around Jonah Beer
Wehle could not help interpreting the event as a foreboding
of the coming of Sabbatai Zevi's second and last successor.

At New Year 5559, when Eleazar Fleckeles thundered against the Sabbateans and Frankists of Bohemia, Bonaparte was in Egypt. The preacher did not mention this event which troubled the minds of those whom he was denouncing.

The sermons of Eleazar Fleckeles and his continuous warnings against the Frankist menace put the community on the alert. Suspicions about the secret meetings in the home of Jonas Beer Wehle and the travels to Offenbach were raised by the numerous fanatical adversaries of Frankism. This campaign finally crystallized in an official denunciation of the Frankists which avowedly was aimed at their prosecution by the authorities. At the beginning of July, 1799, a long anonymous letter, signed B, was delivered to the chief magistrate (*Stadthauptmann*) of Prague, Count Vratislav de Latoure.[38]

The particular feature of the letter is its emphasis on the political significance of the Frankists' activities. The very name "Frank" indicates, in his opinion, the connection with Revolutionary France; Frank's removal to Offenbach is taken as a sign of Frank's sympathy with the French revolutionaries. The writer of the letter finally suggests that the religious sect, indulging in "occult meetings, mystical signs, enthusiasm, and superstition," might be a secret society which, as every society of this kind, "is the pestilence of the state." Not the general behavior of the sect, but disturbing happenings of the most recent days caused the writer to address the letter to the chief magistrate:

> Your Honor may judge for yourself what embarrassment seized the whole Jewish community here when

it was learned with certainty that for the last fourteen
days some of the sect travelled from here to Offenbach — to be sure they pretended for commercial reasons and declared that it was a voyage to Germany —
but this is completely untrue. The travellers are Aaron
Beer Hersch Wehle and Gabriel Porges. By no means
may treason towards the beloved native country be
supposed, for it were ridiculous to assume that such a
little group is able to undertake something serious. It is
merely religious enthusiasm, hope of redemption. The
overturn of the papal throne has already sufficiently
nourished their fancies. Publicly they declared that this
is a sign of the approaching Messiah, for this consti-
tutes their main belief: Sabath Zebe was the Messiah
and remains the Messiah, but always in another form.
*The conquests of the General Bonaparte gave nourish-
ment to their superstitious doctrine. His conquests in
the Orient, particularly the conquest of Palestine, of
Jerusalem, his proclamation to the Israelites is oil on
their flame, and it is believed that this is the very root
of the connection between them and the society of
Frank. However, how? And what for? Who can know
this?* [italics are mine].

These lines represent the only extant Jewish information
about the issue of Bonaparte's Proclamation. The description
of the Proclamation is in accordance with the discovered
text to the "Israelites," and not merely to the Jews of Asia
and Africa; this seems to indicate that the original Proclamation — not the report of the *Moniteur* or of the *Vossische*

Zeitung — was meant by the writer of the letter. A further indication of this fact is the reference to the conquest of Palestine and especially of Jerusalem, which corresponds with the dating and with the pertinent — incorrect — statement of the Proclamation. The letter justifies the assumption that a copy of the Proclamation had reached Prague and came into the hands of the Frankists. This supposition is also corroborated by the date of the anonymous letter: June 27, 1799 — two months and one week after the issue of the Proclamation. Sufficient time for the conveyance of the copy from Palestine to Prague had passed. The letter confirms the assumption that the Proclamation, in spite of its premature date, had been copied and dispatched to the Diaspora. It finally provides the explanation why the only document which contains the complete text of the Proclamation can be traced to Prague.

The date of the letter in relation to that of the Proclamation is indeed the most important key to the historical implications of the anonymous document. The bewilderment of "the whole Jewish community" caused by the departure of three Frankists to Offenbach two weeks earlier, at the beginning of June, 1799, can only be understood when viewed in the light of the excitement which the "Proclamation to the Israelites" had produced in Prague. The people around Wehle from whose meetings information about the Proclamation spread were watched most closely. They had travelled to Offenbach before, and Rabbi Fleckeles had rebuked them because of these visits. But in the situation created by the arrival of the Proclamation the sudden voyage of several prominent members of the Wehle group seemed to give serious cause for alarm. The letter has to be understood as an outcome both of the mistrust of the Sabbateans and of the enormous apprehension called forth by the Proclamation. It reflects the tension which pervaded the ghetto of Prague in Summer 1799. The special emphasis laid by "B" on the patriotic feelings of the Jewish nation indicates the political nature of the dissension between the majority of the Jewish citizens who dissociated themselves categorically from Bonaparte's call and the group of alleged sympathizers with the Proclamation.

The writer of the letter is by no means definite in his statements about the nature of the political convictions and activities of the Sabbateans. Instead of making specific charges, he again and again points to the suspicious travels and the secret meetings of the people around Wehle. He knows of two travellers who "only last Friday returned [from Offenbach] and put up at Jonas Beer Wehle's. One presumes that they have brought with them various writings... It happens also every week that a well-locked small box is sent from Prague to Kolin to a certain Veit Lichtenberg." Only by a swift raid on Saturday at 4 p.m. when the meetings at the homes of Wehle in Prague and Lichtenberg in Kolin took place secretly, could the authorities get hold of the writings.

The surprising appearance of the Proclamation in Prague might have been linked with Offenbach. From the very beginning of the movement, the Frankists maintained connections with Turkey, especially with Salonika. Among the mixed Frankist crowd of Offenbach some former Turkish nationals might have been present. The communications which they maintained with the Orient may have proved useful for the secret conveyance of the Proclamation. Another opportunity of receiving a copy of the document was offered by the vicinity of France.

At any rate no definite conclusions can be drawn either from the letter or from other sources whether or in which manner the Frankists of Prague actually responded to Bonaparte's Proclamation. The pre-Zionism of Jonas Beer Wehle and his followers was most probably couched in terms of Sabbatean Messianism. The allusion of the anonymous author to the confirmation which "their superstitious doctrine" has found in Bonaparte's conquests and in his Proclamation was evidently based on correct observation: the trained cabbalists could hardly help looking upon those momentous events as preliminaries of the approaching redemption.

PART FIVE

THE TEXT OF THE PROCLAMATION REAPPEARS
AFTER ONE HUNDRED AND FORTY-ONE YEARS

17

THE PROCLAMATION IN HISTORICAL LITERATURE

The suppression of the Proclamation by Bonaparte and the silence with which it was observed during the reign of Napoleon were necessarily reflected for a very long time in historical literature. No reference to the report of the *Moniteur* can be found in any of the memoirs based on Napoleon's dictation or conversation on St. Helena. Napoleon's reluctance to stir up the memories of that episode was caused, as has been shown, by the catastrophic reversal of his plans and by the preposterous contents of the Proclamation. Confident that the document had been suppressed, he preferred avoiding the embarrassing subject altogether.

The omission of any reference to the event became indeed a common feature in most modern monographs about the Expedition. They followed the general trend which focused attention upon Egypt and Bonaparte's temporary rule of the land of the pharaohs. This lack of interest in the invasion of Palestine and in Bonaparte's Restorationist experiment found its natural reflex in the biographies of Napoleon. From the standard works by Thiers and Lanfrey up to the master-pieces by Bainville, Fournier, Holland-Rose, and Thompson, the short but most dramatic moment in the early life of their hero when he exchanged the role of Alexander the Great for that of Cyrus has been ignored. The suppression of that episode by the masters of historiography was one of Napoleon's last triumphs.

This elimination of an essential detail of Napoleon's achievements from posterity was aggravated by an emphasis on Napoleon's later dealings with the Jews. In fact, the almost exclusive attention paid to the convocation of the Jewish Notables and of the Great Sanhedrin, coupled with the interpretation of the two Jewish conventions as instruments of assimilation, seemed to obliterate entirely any trace of the Proclamation.

In the end, Jewish historians, anxious to offer a full account of Napoleon's dealings with the Jews, renewed the memory of Bonaparte's attempt to restore Israel. To be sure, the policy of the Emperor Napoleon, above all of the Great Sanhedrin, absorbed their interests for a long time. The assimilationist trend of the Emancipation era diverted attention from Bonaparte's Proclamation to his later activities. Only with the rise of national consciousness did Napoleon's attempt to restore Israel become a subject of Jewish historiography.

Heinrich Graetz set forth the theory that Bonaparte's Proclamation was meant to lure Farhi away from the Turks and the British.[39] Had Bonaparte succeeded in conquering Syria and carrying the war into the heart of Turkey, he would perhaps have assigned a share in his government to members

of the Jewish nation upon which the French could have re-
lied. Graetz was highly critical of Napoleon's rule in general.
He correctly perceived the basic contradictions in Napoleon's
approach to the Jews: his admiration of Israel's indestructi-
bility and his contempt for contemporary Jewry, his resolve
to raise the Jewish nation and his simultaneous oppressive
policy against it. Graetz termed the assemby of the Jewish
Notables "the first Jewish Parliament" and perceived the revivalist motive in Napoleon's policy regarding the Jews. In
fact, the chapters dealing with Napoleon's attitude toward
the Jews are the only parts in the concluding volume in
which Graetz, deviating from his basic principle of calling
the Jews a "tribe" or "national tribe," describes them as a
nation.

In comparison with Graetz, Simon Dubnow was far from
recognizing the revivalist aims that Napoleon and, to some
extent, the members of the Sanhedrin had pursued. There
was, nevertheless, an affinity between Dubnow's views and
the principles of the Napoleonic policy regarding the Jews —
the fundamental idea that the Jews, during the long history
of the Diaspora, had preserved their national character. Likewise, the calling of the Jewish Notables and of the Great
Sanhedrin amounted to a recognition of the autonomy of
the Jewish community at large — Dubnow's favorite notion
and demand. It was, after all, the most ostentatious demon-
stration of self-government that ever took place during the
history of the Diaspora. The Proclamation which, as he
stated, was issued after the capture of Gaza and Jaffa, was
but a political stratagem to ensnare the Jewish population
for the benefit of the Palestinian campaign.[40]

In the meantime, however, a series of attempts had been made to throw more light on the origin and contents of the Proclamation. All these efforts were prompted by the rise of the Zionist movement and by the momentous events which culminated in the issue of the Balfour Declaration and in the creation of the Jewish National Home.

Leon Kahn's account of the relation between Bonaparte's Eastern Expedition and the Jews, "Les Juifs de Paris pendant la Revolution," (1898) was the first elaborate presentation of the subject. Kahn's interest in the problem was, however, not aroused by admiration of Bonaparte or by appreciation of his dealings with the Jews. He was, on the contrary, highly critical of Napoleon's character and particularly of his policy concerning the Jews during the Empire. Kahn admitted that Bonaparte, during the Italian and Oriental campaigns, was not unfavorably disposed toward the Jews, but he condemned the Eastern Expedition as an ambitious enterprise undertaken for Bonaparte's greater glory and the idea of a national Restoration of the Jews as a "chimera" (p. 321).

Leon Kahn was no Zionist. His assimilationist views and French patriotism speak unequivocally from the book. It is, nevertheless, reasonable to assume that the rise of the Zionist idea induced Kahn to break with the habit of bypassing the historic events of 1799, which had become a tradition in the Emancipation era. He remained, in this respect, an isolated phenomenon within French historical literature. When shortly afterward Albert Lemoine published his book, "Napoléon et les Juifs" (1900), only a single rather scant paragraph (on p. 74) dealing with the Syrian campaign was to be found in it. Lemoine did not even mention the Proclamation and supposed that Bonaparte, in order to arouse enthusiasm among the Jews and to win their friendship, spread the rumor of his intention to create a Jewish army and to establish a Jewish kingdom. Lemoine saw in this move only a political maneuver inspired by sheer necessity. Lemoine's negative treatment of Bonaparte's attempt to restore the Jewish people was surpassed by Robert Anchel, the author of *Napoléon et les Juifs* (1928), the classic study devoted to this subject, which is completely silent about Bonaparte's historic move to reestablish the Jewish people in the Land of Israel.

Philip Guedalla, the noted English historian, was the first to treat the Proclamation as a special subject. As the foundation of the Jewish National Home coincided with the centenary of Napoleon's death, a special meeting of the Jewish Historical Society of England was devoted entirely to the theme, "Napoleon in Palestine."

The merit of his lecture consisted in the exposition of the unsolved problems:

> Is it a fact, that the Jews of Asia and Africa were called to arms pour établir l'ancienne Jérusalem...? Had Bonaparte appealed to the Jews in Palestine; or was it only a lie from the French embassy at Constantinople?
>
> The report from Constantinople speaks of a proclamation to the Jews. It is unfortunately true that no such document exists. There are two thousand papers in the correspondence which relate to the Egyptian expedition. They deal with matters of every magnitude, from the

partition of the Turkish empire to the inscriptions on swords of honor for deserving troopers and the supply of forage at distant parts in Upper Egypt; and they include at least one proclamation to Arabs in Palestine. But there is no trace of a proclamation to the Jewish people. Again, two possibilities remain. Either the call to arms was verbal, or a false report was circulated from Constantinople upon Bonaparte's instructions (pp. 27–30).

Once the enigma was formulated, it began to haunt historians. Shortly after the publication of Guedalla's lecture, the historian N. M. Gelber devoted a special chapter to "Napoleon's Project of a Jewish State." He, too, observed with regret that it was difficult to establish the authenticity of the report of the *Moniteur* owing to the fact that the manifesto itself had vanished. He reported on the negative results of his own investigations in the Imperial Archives of Vienna where he had checked the entire diplomatic correspondence, particularly the dispatches of the Austrian representative in Constantinople. Gelber suggested the possibility of discovering relevant documents in the correspondences of other states, above all of England.[41]

In contrast to Guedalla and Gelber, S. D. Weinryb, in a Hebrew article, relegated the whole story of the Proclamation to the realm of legend. The answer to this attempt came from Benzion Dinaburg (Dinur), professor of History at the Hebrew University of Jerusalem. In a thorough study of Bonaparte's Eastern Expedition he rejected Weinryb's view, yet the absence of the Proclamation induced him to put forth the theory that the contents of the Proclamation were identical with that of the *"Letter to the Brethren"* of 1798.[42]

Such was the state of our knowledge when — thanks to an extraordinary combination of circumstances — the missing and long sought for text of the Proclamation came into the hands of the present writer.

18

THE TEXT OF THE PROCLAMATION COMES
TO LIGHT

The occupation of Austria by the Nazis forced me to leave
Vienna in September, 1938, and to settle — after a short stay
in Switzerland — in England. I arrived there in April, 1939,
and took residence in London where I spent a considerable
time in the reading room of the British Museum in studies
of materials for a history of the British Movement for the
Restoration of the Jews to Palestine. I had already dealt
with this subject in my "History of the Jews in Letters from
the East and West" published shortly before my emigration.
A chapter of the book was devoted to Napoleon whose
"Proclamation to the Jews of Asia and Africa" was quoted
according to the report of the *Moniteur*. A reading of Philip
Guedalla's lecture in the British Museum drew my attention
to this event and to the mysterious disappearance of the
original document.

In spring, 1940, a friend of mine, Dr. Ernst Müller, a well-
known scholar and writer, a refugee from Austria like my-

self, suggested that I visit another emigrant from Vienna, Mr. Ernst Foges, a former merchant, whose acquaintance he had made in Vienna. The old gentleman was, as Dr. Müller told me, very anxious to meet me, mainly because he wanted to show me a document on the assumption that I, as a historian and editor of Jewish letters, might be interested in it. The critical situation of those days was not very auspicious for an intensification of social life. I nevertheless made up my mind to see the man — whom I had never met before — and called on him with my wife and co-worker, Dora Kobler, in his apartment in London (136 Hamilton Terrace, N.W.8) on the afternoon of July 4, 1940.

My expectations were definitely surpassed by the impression he made from the very first moment, a man of medium height, with sparkling eyes and a handsome face adorned by a white beard in the style of the Victorian era. Many common interests led at once to a lively conversation. Before long he interjected the remark that I might be interested in a historical document which was in his possession. "What kind of document?" was my obvious question. The answer, "Napoleon's Proclamation to the Jews," though surprising, was not received with particular excitement; I assumed, rather, that Mr. Foges was about to show me a copy of the well-known report of the *Moniteur*. I had hardly uttered my doubts about Foge's announcement, when he took from his desk a piece of paper and handed it to me. It was a square sheet of ordinary thin typewriter-paper, upon both sides of which a German text was typewritten. I looked with astonishment on the inscription which read as follows:

ZUSCHRIFT
AN DIE JUEDISCHE NATION
1. Von dem französischen Obergeneral Buonaparte
2. von Rabbi Aron in Jerusalem
aus *dem Original* übersetzt
1799

LETTER
TO THE JEWISH NATION
1. From the French General-in-Chief Bonaparte
2. From Rabbi Aron in Jerusalem
translated from *the original*
1799

I glanced with rising amazement over the lines covering the two pages and listened spellbound to the explanation of Mr. Foges about the origins of this most intriguing piece of writing:

After the occupation of Austria in 1938, Mr. Foges decided to emigrate and was anxious to bring the inherited family treasures out of the country. These treasures, consisting of pictures, precious old books, and papers, were mainly a heritage left by his maternal grandfather, David Fleckeles, a merchant of Prague. At the approach of danger, Mr. Foges had checked through his library and archives. On this occasion he had found among the posthumous papers of his grandfather an old sheet of sturdy paper with a handwritten German text on both sides. It showed the above-quoted inscriptions and seemed thus to be an interesting document of the Napoleonic era. Mr. Foges made a typewritten copy of the manuscript, while the original document itself was packed with the greater part of his library and papers (among them diaries kept by Mr. Foges himself) for removal to Palestine. Mr. Foges originally intended to settle in Palestine and to present the document as a gift to the Jerusalem Archives. He preferred to bring the document out of Austria together with his other belongings than to carry it with him, because of the danger of its confiscation by the Nazi authorities when they conducted a very thorough bodily inspection of the Jewish emigrants. Later on, however, Mr. Foges — an independent bachelor — abandoned his plan of going immediately to Palestine and took refuge in England. In the meantime, the huge case (a "Liftvan") carrying the No. E.F.157 chg. 1580 had been forwarded by the forwarding house Loob & Schwartz, Vienna, to Trieste with the destination Palestine. After having arrived in Trieste, the case was stored in the store-house of the Lloyd Triestino Italiano (later "Oriens") in August, 1939. Mr. Foges could not make up his mind about having the case forwarded to England, owing to the considerable expense involved because he still contemplated the possibility of going to Palestine. In June, 1940, Italy declared war on Great Britain and the removal became practically impossible. Thus, the belongings of Mr. Foges including the original document, remained in the storehouse for the duration of the war.

Upon my inquiry into his knowledge about the origin of the document, Mr. Foges was able to offer me the first valuable clues. His grandfather David Fleckeles (1802—1864), was the son of Wolf Fleckeles (1775—1849), head of the Jewish community of Prague for thirty years. Wolf's elder brother was Rabbi Eleazar Fleckeles (1754—1826), the eminent Talmudic scholar and preacher of the Napoleonic era. It was, therefore, Mr. Foges' assumption that the document — though its handwriting was, in his opinion, that of Wolf Fleckeles — was originally in the possession of Rabbi Eleazar Fleckeles and passed from him into the hands of Wolf who survived his brother by twenty-five years. The mother of Mr. Foges was Lucy, daughter of David Fleckeles and Henrietta née Janowitzer.

Jonas Wehle and his circle must be considered the primary recipients of Bonaparte's Proclamation and of Rabbi Aaron's covering letter. It is very plausible that these documents were confiscated by the authorities — either Jewish or official — in the public uproar which occurred shortly after the denunciations of "B." Leading figures of both camps were arrested and interrogated; a copy of the subversive and incriminating manuscripts may have been discovered or turned over. In this case they would have reached Carolus Fischer, the censor and official interpreter and a friend of Eleazar Fleckeles. Rabbi Fleckeles most probably received official information about the finds of the authorities from Fischer. This assumption is supported by some features of the extant translation. The inscription itself with its enumeration of the two translated documents seems to indicate an enclosure of official files. If the translation had been prepared for private or historical purposes, no summary of this kind was needed. Likewise, the denomination of the two documents as "Zuschrift" ("letter" in an official sense) is in accordance with an authoritative translation. It is noteworthy that "Aufruf," the only appropriate German word for Bonaparte's

Proclamation, or the usual term "proclamation" itself, have been carefully avoided, although the anonymous informer expressly refers to an "Aufruf an die Israeliten" which stirred the Sabbateans of Prague. Carolus Fischer, or whoever was responsible for the wording of the inscription, obviously tried to minimize the importance of Bonaparte's manifesto by calling it a "Zuschrift" and noting no difference between the documents. The assumption that the extant translation was part of the official files seems to offer an explanation of the missing indication of the language from which the translation was made. A private translator who wanted to prepare a record of the historic document would have mentioned the original language. Such an indication was, however, superfluous in a translation which was a part of the official files containing the original. The official files on the subject, however, have disappeared. At some date in the nineteenth century they were stolen, hidden, or destroyed in order not to compromise or embarrass the descendants of the original Frankists.

An inquiry was addressed to the Lloyd Triestino and was answered by the "Oriens," the successor of the Lloyd on September 5, 1945, with the information that the indicated case had been sequestrated by the Supreme German Commissar on May 8, 1944, for the benefit of the First Mayor of Berlin (*Oberbürgermeister der Reichshaupstadt Berlin*) and handed over to the Supreme Commissar of the Operative Zone Adriatic Coast (*Oberster Kommissär in der Operations-Zone Adriatischers Küstenland*). According to additional information, the case had been opened in Trieste and the contents, as far as they consisted of books, pictures, antiquities, etc., sold on the spot to librarians and antiquarians, while the remainder (clothes, linen, etc.) were sent to Berlin. Thereupon attempts were made with the help of the World Jewish Congress, British Section (Hon. Secretary Dr. A. Steinberg) to secure the assistance of the Jewish community of Trieste in the search for the document. But all the efforts were of no avail.

Ernst Foges (born in Prague, December 17, 1862) died in London on April 24, 1948. Before I left England for the U.S.A., he addressed to me a statement in the German language inscribed *"Die verlorene Handschrift"* (The Lost Manuscript), dated London, January 31, 1947. In it he recorded in a few words the story of how he had found the original manuscript among his old papers, how and why he had prepared the typewritten copy and packed the original, together with other of his belongings in the case ("Lift") destined for Palestine, and how finally the contents of the case, which had remained in Trieste during the war, had been confiscated and disposed of by the Nazi authorities.

19

THE QUESTION OF AUTHENTICITY

The historical reasons for a positive answer to this question have been presented in the preceding chapters. This account shows above all, that a proclamation of the kind which the discovered texts reveal accorded with the political attitude to the Jews which Bonaparte had exhibited in Italy, in Malta, and in Egypt. This uninterrupted sequence of pro-Jewish actions leads to a climax in the Land of Israel of which the Proclamation is a telling expression. It is, moreover, a fair supposition that Bonaparte was acquainted with and influenced by the pre-Zionist *"Letter to the Brethren"* which was published on the eve of the Eastern Expedition, quoted and commented on in *La Décade.* The unearthed texts fit the report of the *Moniteur* and fill the gap which existed previously. It was the lack of documentary proof, the strange fact that no trace of the Proclamation, which (according to the report from Constantinople) had been issued by Bonaparte, was found in his published proclamations or elsewhere, that prompted many to ask whether the Proclamation had not to be dismissed as legend. The discovered documents also offer the clue to the disappearance of the Proclamation and to the even more enigmatic fact that Bonaparte had never once referred to it. Finally, the documentary evidence concerning activities of the Prague Frankists which centered around Bonaparte's Proclamation has confirmed the existence of the Proclamation and provided an explanation why the unearthed texts were found in the hands of the offsprings of a family whose prominent member was intimately connected with the Frankists.

In order to check these historical findings from a different angle, the provenience of the extant translation and the unearthed texts will be subjected to a step-by-step examination on the following pages:

1. Any doubt as to the genuineness of the *typewritten copy*, found in the possession of Ernst Foges, has to be ruled out. His personal account of the preparation of the copy and of the reasons which prompted him to take a transcript of the original translation with him rather than the old sheet itself is as plausible as it is trustworthy.

2. It has thus to be taken for granted that Ernst Foges copied the transcript from the *handwritten manuscript* which consists of, as indicated, a (German) *translation prepared in 1799*. The German texts clearly betray the style of the transition period of the turn of the eighteenth century. Some characteristic words may be quoted, as for instance, *Fersähergeist* ("spirit of seers") instead of *Prophetischer Geist* ("prophetic spirit"); *Nachbahrung* ("proximity") instead of *Nachbarschaft; ahndeten* ("foresaw, felt") instead of *ahnten.* The orthography, too, is in accordance with the practice of the era: thence the use of "y" instead of "i" in words like *bey, seyen,* the use of "h" after "t" in words like

unpartheiische, Erbtheil, the use of "d" in *Schwerdt.* If, in addition, the conclusive fact that David Fleckeles must have inherited the sheet from his father Wolf Fleckeles and the happenings of 1799 in the Prague community, in which Wolf's brother, Eleazar Fleckeles, played such an important role are taken into account, the date 1799 appears sufficiently confirmed.

The same applies to the qualification of the texts as "translation." They present themselves linguistically as renderings from other languages, the covering letter clearly betraying the Hebrew original, while the apparently French original of the Proclamation seems to contain passages which have been translated from the Hebrew into the French. The texts reveal the struggle of the translator with the mixed character of the original. Thus the first word of the opening passage, *Aufmerksamkeit* ("attention") is rather clumsily connected with *und unpartheiische Beobachter* ("and impartial observers"). It is a fair guess that the Hebrew *kavanah* denoting foresight as well as attention or the corresponding adjective has led to this striking inaccuracy. On the other hand, the epithet *jungfräuliche* ("virginal") has been used for the (French) army in literal translation of the French *vierge,* although it does not cover (in German) the metaphoric meaning of "undefiled" or "unconquered." Finally, the strange expression *Fersähergeist* points to the Hebrew word *zofeh* ("seer, prophet") *or zafoh* ("spy, look out").

For all these reasons, there can be no doubt that the hand-written manuscript which Ernst Foges inherited from his grandfather contained a genuine translation of the two documents. As to the identity of the translator and writer of the texts, the first guess was made by Ernst Foges when he added at the end of the transcript the words: "Transcript after the copy (in my archives) probably of my great-grandfather Wolf Fleckeles." Ernst Foges was at that time uniformed about the involvement of Rabbi Eleazar Fleckeles, Wolf's brother, in the struggle with the Frankists of Prague and of the Rabbi's connection with the censor Carolus Fischer.

3. The question of the authorship of the *originals from which the translation was made* (whether the translated records of the Proclamation and of the covering letter were really genuine documents) can logically be asked only by those who have not been convinced by the expounded historical reasons.

a. *Proclamation.* As already pointed out above, the text of the Proclamation contains a series of passages which represent either literal repetitions or variations of utterances which Bonaparte made on other occasions. All of them are of a specific Napoleonic coloring. This applies particularly to the passages that refer to the avenging mission of the French concerning the shame of the remotest nations and to the "war... waged in self-defense." The characterizations of the Jewish Nation in the first apostrophe of the Proclamation and in the order regarding the privileges of the monastery on Mount Sinai offer a most striking analogy. The unique length of Jewish history has been emphasized; a characteristic example of Napoleon's predilection for historical comparisons is the reference to the "brotherly alliance" between the Maccabees and Sparta and Rome.

A precise parallel to the offer to the "Rightful Heirs of

Palestine" is to be found in the letter which Bonaparte addressed to Emir Bashir, Emir of the Druse, on March 20, 1799, only two days after his arrival before Acre. "It is my intention," reads a passage of this letter, "to make the Druse nation independent, to lower the tribute it pays, and to give it the port of Beirut and other towns which it needs as outlets for its commerce." The passage provides evidence that Bonaparte, apart from his fantastic plans of Alexandrian conquests, contemplated a reorganization of the Middle East. The letter to Emir Bashir shows the same resoluteness concerning an unconquered part of the country, as is evidenced in the Proclamation to the Jewish nation regarding Palestine of which he believed he was already an indisputed master.

And yet all these, though very telling, comparisons are overshadowed by the parallelism between the Proclamation to the Jewish nation and a proclamation to another nation issued by Napoleon ten years *after* the call to the "Rightful Heirs of Palestine." On May 13, 1809, he occupied Vienna and established his headquarters in the Imperial palace of Schönbrunn. With a speed reminiscent of the precipitated issue of the Proclamation to the Jewish nation. Napoleon composed and issued a proclamation to the Hungarians on May 15.

Written in three languages — French, German, Hungarian — the call to the Hungarian nation offers an example of that polyglot method which most probably was applied in the appeal to the dispersed people. Moreover, the considerable length of the proclamation is equal to the appeal to the Jews. The similarity of the two documents extends even to the division of the texts into paragraphs of almost the same size and to such details as the twice repeated apostrophe of the two nations. The specific rhetoric of Napoleon dictating could hardly manifest itself more clearly than by these emphatic repetitions. After having addressed himself at the beginning of the proclamation to the "Rightful Heirs of Palestine," and to the Hungarians, he turned to them for a second and third time in the same manner.

An uninterrupted chain of surprising analogies is offered:

Imperial Headquarters in Schönbrunn
15 March 1809

Hungarians!
The Emperor of Austria, unfaithful to his treaties, mistook the magnanimity which I have shown to him in three successive wars, especially after the war of 1805; he has attacked my armies; I have met this attack. God, the Giver of Victory, who punished the ungrateful and the perjurer, has been favorable to my arms; I have occupied the capital and I am standing on your borders. It is the Emperor of Austria, not the King of Hungary, who has declared war against us. By your Constitution he had no right to do so without your consent...

Hungarians! The moment has come to recover your independence. I offer you peace, the integrity of your territory, your liberty and your constitution... I want nothing from you, only to see you free and independent. Your union with Austria has been your misfortune. Your blood has flowed for her on distant fields, and your foremost interests have been continually sacrificed to those of his hereditary States. You formed the fairest portion of the monarchy, and yet were reduced to the position of a subject province and made the sport of passions to which you were strangers; you have your national customs and a national language; you boast of an ancient and illustrious origin. Regain, therefore, your national existence. Become what you were. Have a king of your own choice who reigns you only, who resides in your midst, who is surrounded only by your citizens and your soldiers. Hungarians! this is what Europe, which has its eyes on you, asks of you. This is all I ask of you: a lasting peace, trade relations with me, an assured independence: this is the fair prize that awaits you, if you want to be worthy of your ancestors and of yourselves.

You will not refuse these liberal and generous offers, you will not squander your blood in the causes of feeble Princes, ever dominated by corrupt ministers who are in the pay of England, that enemy of the Continent, which has founded its prosperity on monopoly and on our divisions.

Meet, therefore, in your national Diet in the plains of Rákos, as your ancestors did and let me know the results of your deliberations.

NAPOLEON

Once again the war is declared to be a defensive one, the victory of the French arms is ascribed to Divine Grace, Napoleon reminds the addressed nation of her glorious past and ancient origin and, above all, he emphatically refers to the auspicious moment to seize the favorable opportunity. There exists an almost literal identity of the appeals:

PROCLAMATION TO THE JEWISH NATION	PROCLAMATION TO THE HUNGARIAN NATION
Now is the moment... to claim the restoration of civic rights... your political existence as a nation among nations, and the unlimited right to worship Yehovah.	*The moment has come to recover your independence... Regain, therefore, your national existence. Become what you were.*

Moreover, the form of an offer is again used, though obviously not of a land, but of a series of political benefits listed in the same cumulative manner as the rights which had been offered to the Jewish nation. The promise of independence is present in both proclamations: Jews were reminded of Maccabean glories and exhorted to emulate the allies of Sparta and Rome, the Hungarians were asked to be worthy of their ancestors and to renew the ancient custom of electing their own king on the plains of Rákos.

It is, in fact, the historical coloring of both proclamations which lends to them the Napoleonic mark. From the first to the last line the two calls are permeated by Napoleon Bonaparte's innate passion for history.

There is, finally, *one* feature common to both documents, that nobody but Napoleon could impart to them. In both cases a vehement attack on Napoleon's most dangerous enemy, England, is prominent. In the call to the continental Hungarian nation, England, "that enemy of the Continent," is blamed for having built up its riches on the monopoly of commerce and on the discord of the European nations. In the Proclamation, Napoleon alluded unequivocally to the English nation by an invective against the enemies who regarded the hereditary lands of France as plunder to be divided arbitrarily, and even more distinctly by contrasting the French nation, which does not trade with lands and men, with those who indulge in this practice.

It may be justified to sum up the foregoing comparative examination of the two proclamations by the statement that Napoleon has, by the conception and formulation of his appeal to the Hungarians, provided the evidence for the authenticity of his call to the Jewish nation.

b. *The covering letter of Rabbi Aaron son of Levi* differs in contents and in style from the Proclamation. It consists of biblical quotations and references. Owing to the impossibility of identifying its author, no comparison with other writings is possible, but the peculiarity of the writer and the particular *genius loci* make themselves clearly felt. In the latter respect the choice of the biblical references with their allusions to the actual happenings as the siege of Acre and to the battle at Mount Tabor point definitely to a person immediately involved in the warlike events. Particularly the identification of Bonaparte with Gideon could hardly be conceived by somebody who was not a witness of the victory of the numerically inferior French army over the huge Arab hosts in the plain of Jezreel.

4. In view of all these facts, an assumption that the originals on which the unearthed translation of the two texts has been based were forged documents would presuppose that

he who undertook the falsifications was acquainted: a) with the military situation which preceded the issue of the Proclamation; b) with the outward form of Bonaparte's proclamations; c) with the specific style and spirit of these calls; also that he was an outstanding student of history and an accomplished Hebrew scholar, so excellently versed in French and Hebrew, that he was able to produce the two documents in the short time between the arrival of the news about the issue of Bonaparte's Proclamation and the denunciation of the Frankists by the anonymous informer. But even if such a prodigy was to be found in Prague or elsewhere, willing to take the risk of being accused of subversive activities, it would still remain an enigma why he dared to forge a proclamation of the most famous contemporary in the latter's lifetime, an official document easily disproved.

Apart from all these considerations, it would remain inconceivable for what reason and purpose the text of the Proclamation would have been fabricated, since the important fact of its issue was attested by the report from Constantinople. And — lastly — what could prompt anybody to produce two documents which had to remain hidden, never to be published or otherwise made known?

No additional proof for the authenticity of the two texts is necessary. And yet another very stringent evidence had been provided — by Napoleon's own subsequent policy toward the Jews.

PART SIX

THE ORGANIZATION OF THE JEWISH NATION

20

THE CONVOCATION OF THE JEWISH ETATS GENERAUX

The superhuman activities between the eighteenth Brumaire, 1799 and May 18, 1804, the day when Napoleon assumed the title of Emperor, seemed to have carried him an infinite distance from the Oriental dreams of his youth. Marengo and the Peace of Amiens, the Concordat and the *Code,* the *Université impériale and the Légion d'Honneur* — was such an array of deeds not bound to obliterate the memory of the great adventure which had turned into the greatest failure? Everything had, indeed, gone wrong in Egypt since Bonaparte had left for France: from Kléber's assassination to the defeat of the French by the British — the last disaster that had befallen the expeditionary corps in the East. It is therefore clear that the explicit treatment of the Jewish question was destined for a temporary postponement. In a session of the State Council in 1801, when, at the end of the negotiations about the Concordat, Napoleon, referring to the Jews, declared: "They are a particular nation whose sect does not mix with any other; we will have therefore to deal with them later on." A strong emotional experience was needed in order to rearouse his interest in the Jewish people.

After the battle of Austerlitz, Napoleon returned triumphantly to Paris and on the way he stopped at Strasbourg
on January 22 and 23, 1806. The prefect of the city and the
representatives of the Alsatian country-folk denounced the
Jews to the Emperor for their vicious usurious practices.
The Christian inhabitants of a French province were asking
him for protection against the pretended economic oppres-
sion of Jews who already enjoyed equal rights. His conviction that the Jews constituted a distinct nation was immediately related to an assumption which the denunciation
seemed to support; the distinctiveness of the Jews alienated
them from the gentile population and made the latter their
obvious prey. Napoleon took the complaints against the
Jews at face value. Not only did he lack any knowledge of
the real state of affairs — the merits and risks of agricultural
credit — but his dislike of businessmen, financiers, merchants
and bankers — he used to qualify them altogether as usurers
and thiefs — made him most susceptible to the charges levelled against the Jews of Alsace.[43]

On March 6, 1806, he addressed a note to the Supreme
Judge Régnier in which he asked the legislative section to
examine whether it would be possible not only to declare
all previous mortgages taken by Jews to be null and void,
but also to deprive Jews of their citizenship. Napoleon, in
a postcript, added that the restrictions should be "particularly" applied to Jews who during the last ten years arrived
from Poland and Germany.[44] Signed by Napoleon himself,
the letter to Régnier seems to erase everything which Bonaparte stood for.

From the moment Napoleon took the initiative in the

Jewish question, intensive studies were inaugurated in the State Council and in the Ministry of Justice and the Interior in order to prepare the documentary material for the full deliberation of the Council. At the same time, Napoleon entrusted the task of writing a comprehensive discourse about the policy concerning the Jews to Louis-Matthieu Comte de Molé, then a young man of twenty-five, who, by his *Essai de Morale et de Politique,* published in 1806, had gained a reputation and Napoleon's favor. Molé's political views, above all about the Jews, were in agreement with the opinions of arch-conservative emigrés like Chateaubriand and de Bonald. His memorandum, which he presented to the State Council, reflected the anti-Jewish ideas of this group. It set forth the theory that the Jewish nation had not been forced to practice usury by historical circumstances and had not merely tolerated this practice but that it had been ordered by Moses and the principal Rabbis for the very purpose of separating the Jews from the other nations. Usury was a vice inherent in the character of the Jew to such a degree that no power on earth would be able to extirpate it. Molé concluded that the Jews would have to be subjected to exceptional laws.[45]

In order to counteract Molé's opinions, Jacques Claude Beugnot, one of the counsellors, was charged with the task of giving *his* views. Beugnot, a participant in the Revolution who had been imprisoned during the Reign of Terror, was an able administrator and represented the liberal wing of the State Council. His memorandum found that the total amount of obligations which were contracted by the Jews was not alarming and stated that the Christian moneylender rivals the Jews in rapacity. A remedy against usury could

therefore, he argued, be sought only in the intervention of
the courts. Beugnot also rejected the imposition of a mora-
torium on the debts of Christians to Jews. There was another
fundamental difference between the two memoranda: Molé's
discourse emphasized the national character of the Jews,
while Beugnot evidently dismissed the notion of a Jewish
nation. Jews, as far as they were French citizens, enjoyed,
in his opinion, full equality and protection.

At a session of the Council held in the second half of
April, 1806, a resolution was passed in which Beugnot's
views were approved and reformulated: Usury was to be
eradicated by a law applicable to the whole country and to
all inhabitants. Aware of Napoleon's determination to take
harsh steps against the usurious practices of the Jews, the
members of the Council tried to reach a compromise by the
proposal of a one-year suspension of the debts which Christians owed to Jews. Thus, with the two contesting reports
on the table of the State Council, the scene was set for the
appearance of the Emperor himself.

The full session of the State Council took place on April
30, 1806, at St. Cloud. It was Beugnot's first opportunity to
speak before the Emperor. Instead of making his point in
the usual maner, Beugnot spoke with great emphasis and
ostentation. He called Molé's report an instrument of the
anti-philosophical coterie which had made the Jewish question a matter of prejudice. Finally, he not only rejected any
exceptional measures against the usurious practices of the
Jews, but called such a step "a lost battle on the battlefields
of Justice." No expression could have been more malapropos
in the presence of the "invincible" Napoleon, none could

have been more improper in connection with the Jews. The reference to a lost battle awakened suppressed memories and thus added to the fury which its true meaning and Beugnot's report had caused. An eyewitness, the young Baron de Barante, recorded the scene:

> When he [Beugnot] finished, the Emperor with a vigor and a more than ordinary vivacity replied to the discourse of M. Beugnot, sometimes mockingly, sometimes in rage. He protested against the theories, against general and absolute principles, against people for whom facts counted for nothing, who sacrificed reality to abstractions. He resumed the unhappy phrase of the lost battle, and, in steadily growing excitement, he began to swear, something which, to my knowledge, never happened to him in the State Council.

The Emperor revealed his final decision to the State Council on May 7, 1806:

> It has been proposed to me to expel the vagrant Jews who are not worthy of French citizenship and to ask the tribunals to make use of discretionary power against usury; but these measures would be insufficient. The Jewish nation has been constituted since Moses, usurious and oppressive. This is not so with the Christians: usurers form an exception among them and are despised. It is therefore not by means of metaphysical laws that the Jews will have to be regenerated; it will be necessary to introduce simple laws in this case, laws of exception.

Napoleon, in spite of the distorted views he held about the Jewish national character, tried to reconcile discriminatory legislation with the dignity of the Jewish people:

> One must prohibit commerce to the Jews because they misuse it, in the same way as one prohibits the trade of a goldsmith who falsifies gold. Metaphysics have misled the speaker [*i.e.*, Beugnot] so much that he preferred a violent measure of deportation to a more effective and milder remedy... That law needs a foundation. It is necessary to assemble the "étas généraux" of the Jews, that is to summon fifty or sixty to Paris and to hear them. I wish that a General Synagogue be held in Paris on June 15.

Napoleon stressed not only the national character of the Jews but also their historical continuity and uniqueness. This aspect is the very point of departure of his new policy regarding the Jews: specific treatment of this very peculiar people, not the application of general — "metaphysical" — principles. Napoleon had once tried to regenerate this people on its own soil, now another task was before him: To correct them. The summons of the Jewish etats généraux was, under the given circumstances, the proper way to reaffirm his recognition of the Jewish nation and to express, at the same time, his confidence in its regenerative forces.

21

THE ASSEMBLY OF JEWISH NOTABLES —
THE FIRST JEWISH PARLIAMENT

Heinrich Graetz has called the Assembly which was constituted according to the Decree of May 30, 1806, the first
Jewish Parliament. Never before in Jewish history had a
gathering taken place like the meeting of the 111 Jewish
delegates from France and Italy. The delegates were not
chosen by the people whom they represented but were selected by the prefects, and thus a body after the pattern which
was generally practiced in the Empire came into being. To
be sure, the Divan Bonaparte had formed in Cairo might
have been the prototype of an assembly which was to deal
with religious as well as political matters. The directives
given in the decree to the prefects indicate clearly that a
representation of the religious leaders and of the "laymen,"
and among the latter, of the well-to-do and of the educated
elements was intended.

At any rate, an examination of the leading personalities
among the delegates shows that worthy spokesmen of the
main trends had been chosen by the prefects. Orthodox Judaism was represented by the outstanding French rabbi and
scholar, Joseph David Sinzheim of Strasbourg. Among the

conservative delegates were the Portuguese rabbi Abraham Andrade of Saint-Esprit and two Italian rabbis, Graziado Nepi and Jacob Israel Carmi of Reggio. Sinzheim's counterpart among the modernist rabbinical delegates was the distinguished Italian Rabbi Abraham Vita di Cologna, a member of the Italian parliament. Among the laymen an array of well-known revolutionary fighters for the rights of the Jews were ready to participate in the new struggle for the Jewish cause. Two men stood in the forefront: Isaac Berr Berr, the doughty defender of the Alsatian Jews, and the champion of the Portuguese Jews, Abraham Furtado of Bordeaux. Furtado was one of the four deputies of the Jews of Bordeaux who presented to the National Assembly in 1789 a petition for the abolition of Jewish disabilities. A particularly imposing deputation came from Alsace and the other eastern departments, where the Jews had recently been the object of vehement attacks.

The delegates were summoned by the Minister of the Interior to the first session of the Assembly to be held in the Hôtel de Ville. That day happened to be a Saturday. The fact plunged the deputies into a serious conflict. The main item of the order of the day was the election of the president and of a secretary. The votes were to be cast in writing, which meant desecration of the Sabbath. At a private preparatory debate on the critical situation Isaac Berr Berr and his followers joined the rabbis who advocated the postponement of the session or at least of the elections. The modernists, however, deemed it necessary to demonstrate, by yielding to the imperial demand, that Jews respect the formal laws. After a stormy debate a resolution was passed to comply fully with the request of the Emperor. Thus, on July 25, 1806, Paris witnessed the strange scene of the Jewish deputies gathering in the aptly decorated Chapel of St. John of the Hôtel de Ville. It came as a shock to the Orthodox that several deputies arrived in carriages, but when a last minute attempt to postpone the session failed, the proceedings took place without a further incident. Rabbi Lipmann of Colmar, the senior member, presided at the election of the President.

The Emperor had ordered that a guard of honor be placed before the hall of the Assembly. When the Assembly was closed the commanding officer approached the president and asked for his orders. The guard presented military honors to the delegates as they left the Hôtel de Ville. Such a procedure was an unprecedented event in Jewish history. Modelled after the pattern of the military honors which had been offered to the Egyptian dignitaries and to the Divan of Cairo, the official respect shown to the Jewish Assembly was an unmistakable gesture symbolizing the political recognition of the Jewish people. The political treatment of the Assembly was confirmed by an additional outward sign: Special headdress and swords were allotted to the delegates and the guards were ordered to salute them on the streets.

The Emperor did not communicate directly with the Jewish Assembly but made provision for the representation of his personal views. The appointment of Molé to the office of the first of three special imperial commissars indicated that Napoleon wished to emphasize his own critical attitude. Molé's principal role must, however, not overshadow the activities of the two other commissars: Joseph Marie Portalis, the son of the Minister of Cults, and Etienne Denis

Pasquier, who were liberal-minded and well disposed towards the Jews. Their opposition to Molé was manifest and led to almost constant disagreements. The composition of the board of commissars thus reflected the intrinsic conflict in Napoleon's own mind regarding the Jews. Since he had to resume the solution of the Jewish question, he was agitated by its inherent contradictions. Pasquier in particular was confident that he comprehended the Emperor's true intentions:

> When the time came for us to take cognizance of our instructions (I am speaking of M. Portalis and myself) we could not help realizing that the whole drift of the Emperor's ideas had not been fully grasped, and that M. Molé and the State Council had failed to penetrate his thoughts. It was plain that the Emperor's objective was to perform a great political act out of what was being looked upon merely as a measure of oppression. In fact, the question at issue, according to the documents submitted to us, was to ascertain from the Jews themselves, if their religion really permitted them to take up citizenship in such countries as were ready to grant it to them; whether that religion did not embody prescriptions which rendered impossible, or least very difficult, an entire submission for the laws. Lastly, whether there were any means by which it were possible to turn to the advantage of society as a whole the talents of a population which so far had shown itself its avowed enemy.[46]

In accordance with Napoleon's instructions, a questionnaire was submitted to the Assembly. The questionnaire comprised twelve questions of which the first three dealt with marriage law, the fourth, fifth, and sixth with relations of the Jews to Frenchmen and France, the seventh and eighth with the rights and jurisdiction of the rabbis, the tenth with the professions which Jewish law forbids, and the last two questions with the permissibility of usury in dealing with Jews and non-Jews. There is no certainty that Napoleon was the author of this document. Pasquier, in the passage quoted above, seems to indicate that the questionnaire was indeed the emperor's own work. Even if, as is likely and has often been supposed, Molé participated in the draft of the questionnaire, Napoleon has to be credited with the principal share in its composition. It was under his guidance that the document assumed the character of a legislative scheme.

Napoleon was among the champions of the new ways of Jewish life. In the Proclamation of 1799 he had praised the Maccabean heroes "whose brotherly alliance did honor even to Sparta and Rome". Now Napoleon, identifying the new French Empire with imperial Rome, tried to bring about a partnership of the Jewish people with the French nation. Under these impressions Napoleon formulated the principal questions (4 to 6) to the Jewish Notables:

4. Do the Jews regard Frenchmen as their brethren or as aliens?

5. In either case what conduct does their law prescribe toward Frenchmen who are not of their religion?

6. Do the Jews who were born in France and whom

> French law treats as French citizens regard France
> as their fatherland?
>
> Are the Jews obligated by their laws to defend
> France, to obey her laws, and to conform to all
> provisions of the Civil Code?

Viewed in the light of the fifteen years which had passed
since civil equality had been granted to the Jews of France,
the questions would seem preposterous and even provoca-
tive. In order to understand the meaning of the questions
they must not be related to the Jews as individuals; they
refer, by implication, to the Jews of France as a part of the
Jewish people. The French National Assembly in granting
complete equality in 1791 had not been interested in this
relation. For Napoleon, however, the Jewish nation continued to be a living entity even after emancipation, and the
question whether such an adherence was compatible with
the exercise of civic rights remained a vital issue. Although
he shared the general misinformation of the era about Judaism, he realized the indissolubility of the Jewish religion
and the Jewish people. He was also aware of the authority
which Jewish law still exercised over the bulk of Jewry. His
concern was not whether Jews, without regard to their law,
were prepared to comply with the requirements of French
citizenship, but whether their religious law was in conformity
with these obligations.

Thus, the Notables were not asked whether the Jews considered themselves a separate nation but whether their supposed national existence could be reconciled, according to

the valid Jewish law, with the exigencies of an immediate and all-embracing participation in the life of a non-Jewish nation. The question of whether the Jews regarded Frenchmen as their berthren or as aliens did; therefore, by no means concern the feelings of single Jewish men and women. It was a question of supernational law and politics referring to the Jews in general, not merely to the French Jews. It would also be quite erroneous to understand it in the sense of pointing to an identification of Jews with Frenchmen. One could rather recognize in the question a reflex of Napoleon's wish to achieve a "brotherly alliance" of the sort which he had praised in the Proclamation. The subsequent question — whether the French Jews regarded France as their fatherland seems to be separated by an abyss from the Proclamation which invited the Jews to take possession of Israel's patrimony. But the gap between the two pronouncements diminishes considerably at closer examination. Napoleon's question does, in fact, clearly indicate that France can claim to be the fatherland of the Jews, who have been born there, only on the account of treating them as French citizens and thus removing — in the words of the Proclamation — "the two-thousand-year-old ignominy" put upon them. Again, it is not the individual Jew but a part of the Jewish nation that has acquired a fatherland. And only under this aspect does the next question make sense. For obviously the French law was sufficient to secure the defense of France, the obedience to the laws and the conformity to all provisions of the Civil Code by the Jews if they were regarded as French citizens. What prompted Napoleon to raise the question whether the system of the Code Civil and the Jewish law could be har-

monized was the silent recognition of the French Jews as
a part of the Jewish nation living under "their laws."

The Emperor did not use the word "nation" in the questionnaire. There is a contrast between the omission of this
expression and the emphasis with which he had used it not
only in the Proclamation but also during the deliberations
about the convocation of the Assembly. But it was apparently as a part of that process which transformed his original
oppressive intentions into an extraordinary act of statesmanship that Napoleon also reshaped the language of his new
policy. There is, above all, reason to assume that the Proclamation worked as a phychological inhibition against the
public and official use of an expression which had formed
the keynote of the ill-fated manifesto. While he felt bound
to basic conceptions about the Jewish nation, he was eager
to appear neutral in the impending debate. Thus, the questions which he put before the Jewish Notables assume the
character of an inquiry into the essence of Jewish nationhood at the doorstep of the Emancipation era.

The questionnaire was presented to the Assembly in a
solemn session on July 29, 1806. The deputies listened in
breathtaking silence to Molé's reading of the twelve questions. Only once was the silence interrupted when they were
asked whether Jews who are born in France were obliged
by their law to defend France, several deputies, some of
whom had participated in the wars of the Republic, simultaneously exclaimed: "Unto death!" The Assembly appointed a committee for the preparation of the answers to
the twelve questions. The committee entrusted the main preparatory work to the learned Rabbi David Sinzheim who

emerged as the towering figure of the Assembly. He succeeded in completing the answers within the astoundingly
short period of five days.

With complete unanimity the Notables settled the fundamental problem of the questionnaire: the relation of the
Jews to the French and to France. They declared that the
Jews regard the French as their brethren and not as aliens;
this attitude was, they pointed out, rooted in the Jewish
religion which teaches the brotherhood of all men who recognize God as creator of heaven and earth. An even more
emphatic answer was given to the question whether Jews
who were born in France and whom French law treats as
citizens regard France as their fatherland:

> The love of the fatherland is, among the Jews, such a
> natural, such a vivid sentiment and so much in con-
> formity with their religious faith that a French Jew
> regards himself in England even amidst other Jews, as
> a stranger, and the same applies to an English Jew in
> France.

The answer of the Notables to the question concerning the
relation of the French Jews to France betrays their frantic
effort to dispell any doubts about their patriotism. They
tried, in fact, to outdo Napoleon's own intentions. Whereas
he had indicated that the Jews should recognize France as
their fatherland only if French laws treat them as citizens,
the answer of the Asembly declared that the Jews adopted
France as their fatherland even in times when they were
deprived of civil equality. The Notables, asked whether they
regard Frenchmen as their brethren, hastened to declare

themselves Frenchmen. Finally, not satisfied even with this confession, they found it necessary to assure the Emperor that they regard Jews of other countries as strangers, choosing the English Jews as an appropriate example.

The Notables succeeded by their procedure both in vindicating the Jewish people and in manifesting its national existence. We have the telling testimony of Pasquier about the deep impression which the first Jewish Parliament produced on those who until then had not seen Judaism in action:

> It had been generally supposed that they [*i.e.*, the Jews] were governed solely by their pecuniary interests, that they adhered to their religion merely as a matter of custom, and especially because it made their conscience feel easy on the score of living at the expense of all countries which harbored them or tolerated their presence. But one found oneself, face to face with men vastly superior to the common herd with which, generally speaking, public opinion classed them. Thoroughly conversant with their religion and its principles, they were strengthened in their attachment to it by the animadversion it drew upon them, and their well-cultivated minds were replete with every kind of knowledge. *It was therefore no longer possible to ignore the existence of a Jewish nation* [Italics are mine], the dregs of which had so far along come under notice, and which, owing to the care bestowed in selecting the members of the Assembly, spoke a language worthy of being listened to.[47]

Soon after the approval of the answers by the Assembly, Napoleon's thirty-seventh birthday was celebrated in Paris. On that day — August 15 — the delegates assembled in the synagogue; three of the rabbis delivered sermons in praise of the Emperor — in French, in Italian, and in German. Special hymns composed for this occasion by two of the deputies were sung in Hebrew and French. They glorified, among the achievements of the Emperor, his unsurpassed military deeds including those which he performed in Egypt — they did not mention that he had once stood before the walls of Jerusalem and had fought a battle at Mount Tabor.

22

NAPOLEON SUMMONS THE GREAT SANHEDRIN
OF PARIS

The change in Napoleon's intention concerning the Jewish nation was closely linked with a development he himself had experienced. In the past seven years he had definitely ceased to be a Corsican. The ardent patriot of the Mediterranean island had become fervently attached to his new motherland, France. His affection for France became mysteriously blended with his dream to create a new, a vaster empire of Charlemagne. Napoleon's attention was not focused on the restoration of the dispersed people of Israel. Instead of its return to the ancient homeland its integration within his growing empire became his concern. Paris, which he was about to transform into the center of his universal empire, was to become another Jerusalem of a regenerated Jewish nation.

The vision of thus becoming another Solomon or Herod of the Jewish nation was, however, coupled with an even more exalted ambition — of acting like a second Moses for the dispersed people. Another code was to be written: a new law for the Jews of a new epoch. What he had accomplished with respect to Roman law and the Royal Ordinance, he was determined to undertake in the realm of Jewish religious law. For this purpose Napoleon envisaged cooperation be-

tween him and the revived Great Sanhedrin. He planned the
latter not only as a legislative instrument but, at the same
time, as an all-embracing representation of the "universalité
des Israélites." In Pasquier's words:

> His intention was that all the synagogues of the Empire
> and even of Europe should be invited to send to this
> Sanhedrin doctors or delegates who were to unite with
> the Assembly already in existence. Thus, he argued,
> one could flatter oneself with possessing the most legal
> representation of the Jewish religion and nation. This
> would be tantamount to a *resurrection of this nation*
> [Italics mine], which could not fail to see the import-
> ance of being worthy of so signal a boon.

A note addressed to the Minister of the Interior by the Emperor and dated at Rambouillet on August 23, 1806, decreed
that a Great Sanhedrin, a general assembly of Jews, legally
and freely united and embracing Spanish, Portuguese, Italian,
German and French Jews representing more than three quarters of Europe should exercise the right of legislation. Its
acts should be placed beside the Talmud and, while preserving the essential character of the laws of Moses, would
be adapted to the present situation of the Jews, as well as
to French morals and habits. Napoleon simultaneously prescribed the issue of a proclamation which would be officially
communicated to the synagogues of France and of Europe.
The note also contained secret instructions for the commissars. Commenting upon the answers of the Assembly, Napoleon expressed the wish that the Sanhedrin would, as the
Assembly already had done, establish the principle that

Frenchmen and Jews are brethren and that likewise the
Jews are brethren of the inhabitants of all those countries
where they enjoy not only toleration and protection, but
where they are admitted to all civil and political privileges.
Such a declaration would point to the difference between
French and Italian legislation and the legislation of the other
countries. It was also Napoleon's wish that the Sanhedrin
declare that the Jews are obliged to defend France as they
defended Jerusalem, because they are treated in France as
if they were in the Holy Land. The commissars were instructed to impress upon the members of the Assembly the
feeling "that I desire to employ all means in order to bring
it about that the rights which have been restored to the Jewish people may not become illusory and finally to make
them find *Jerusalem in France* [Italics mine]."[48]

The task of reconstituting the historical Sanhedrin was
taken up by the commissars with great zeal. Even Molé was
fascinated by the project, "one of the most beautiful designs
ever conceived for the good of humanity." He prepared, in
the course of a few days, a study about the original Sanhedrin of Jerusalem and presented it to the Minister of the
Interior on September 2, 1806. On the next day, Napoleon
himself addressed from Saint Cloud a note to the minister
giving exact instructions about the procedure for the establishment of the Sanhedrin. The Asembly of Notables, he explained, was to be preserved and augmented by thirty newly-
selected rabbis. The enlarged Asembly would thus constitute
"the assembly of the representatives of the heads of the
Jewish nation, while the Sanhedrin would form a Committee
of the Assembly," its membership being composed of forty

rabbis including fifteen rabbis of the Assembly and a minority of laymen. These precautions show that the Sanhedrin
was bound to preconceived resolutions in accordance with
the intentions of the Emperor.

A committee of nine elected according to Napoleon's request, assisted by Sinzheim, at once prepared the text of the
proclamation to the Universalité of Jews. It was adopted by
the Assembly on September 24 and issued in four languages — Hebrew, French, German and Italian — on October 4 (Tishri 24) fixing the opening of the Sanhedrin on
October 20. Thus, what the Proclamation of 1799 had failed
to achieve, the convocation of the Great Sanhedrin had
brought about. For the first time the Jews officially and
publicly raised their voices in response to a call of Napoleon:

> The benevolence of the Almighty has evidently mani-
> fested itself on us. A great event is being prepared.
> What our ancestors did not see in the course of many
> centuries, what we ourselves could not expect to witness
> in our own days, will reappear before the eyes of an
> astonished world. The 20th October is the day which
> has been fixed for the opening of a Great Sanhedrin
> in the capital of one of the mightiest Christian empires
> and under the protection of an immortal prince who
> reigns there. Paris will then offer this spectacle to the
> world and that for ever memorable happening will
> inaugurate for the dispersed remnants of Abraham's
> posterity a period of salvation and happiness...[49]

The Proclamation of the Notables to European Jewry was

issued during the Emperor's absence from France. Once again Napoleon's interference in the destiny of the Jews coincided with a decisive turn in his own life. Prussia, after having joined the Third Coalition, challenged Napoleon by mobilizing her army. The victorious campaign against Prussia and the one against Russia which followed kept Napoleon outside France for ten months. It is difficult to ascertain to what extent Napoleon's absence from Paris during this period and his preoccupation with other affairs affected the Sanhedrin. Though he did not lose sight of the Sanhedrin and cared for it from afar, the opportunity for his participation in the proceedings and especially for a meeting with the delegates was lost.

The turmoil caused by the hostilities, in which a great part of Europe was involved, offered a serious obstacle to the expected effect of the proclamation to the synagogues. The governments of countries not under the direct or indirect rule of France would hardly have permitted Jews to leave for Paris in order to cooperate with a Jewish legislative body created upon Napoleon's bidding. Austria, with her large and differentiated Jewish population, not only issued a ban against participation in the Sanhedrin but introduced a strong censorship of the correspondence between the Jews of the Austrian provinces and those under French domination. The Jews of Prussia were by no means inclined to promote an idea patronized by the man who had just inflicted a humiliating defeat upon their fatherland. The proclamation of the Jewish Asembly was utterly lost on the Jews of Eastern Europe; the war of France against Russia made the existing obstacles practically insurmountable. Thus French and Italian

Jews continued to dominate the enlarged Jewish Assembly
from which the members of the Great Sanhedrin were to be
chosen. They were joined by five delegates from Holland
and Germany.

The effect of the proclamation which the Jewish Assembly
issued must, not, however, be judged solely by the number
of the foreign delegates. The plan to re-establish the ancient
legislative body of Israel caused a sensation everywhere.
Many letters sent from Jews living in the French empire and
preserved through the interceptions of foreign authorities
show the extravagant hopes caused by the move of Napoleon.
A letter addressed in September, 1806, by Rabbi Popper of
Mainz to his relatives in Teplitz expressed the hope that
Napoleon intended to give back to the Jews all the rights
they enjoyed before the defeat inflicted upon them by Titus.[50]
Another correspondent, writing in October from Hagenau
in Hesse, to a relative in Bohemia, took it for granted that
Napoleon contemplated the settlement of Jews in places
where they had never lived before.[51] Enlightened Jewish
circles in Germany led by the financier Israel Jacobsohn felt
elated by the news from France.

With the war against Russia in its initial stages and the
blockade of England in full swing, the political considerations which had played a part in the idea of reviving the
Great Sanhedrin gained momentum. Napoleon had become
disappointed in his hopes of finding support among the nations of Eastern Europe. The Poles particularly failed to
respond to his call to the extent which he had expected. Thus
the action which he had initiated to win the Jews over to
his side assumed actual importance. The services of the dis-

persed people had never been more desirable than in that moment. The very dispersion offered incomparable opportunities. Jewish merchants could and did help to provide his troops with all sorts of goods and the assistance of Jewish financiers was expected in the economic battle against England. The scheme he had devised on August 23 in Rambouillet seemed adapted to the purpose of obliging the Jews to such services. Had he not offered the Jewish people a new constitution and assured them his protection in the enjoyment of all civil and political rights and offered them "Jerusalem in France" in exchange for the guarantee that the principle of a new Jewish Code would be observed? It was this design which fascinated the originator of *Code Napoléon*. Here was a project as daring as his offer of Palestine to the Jewish nation had been. He felt a personal responsibility for its realization. The note of Rambouillet had been only a suggestion to the Assembly of the Jewish Notables. Now, with the Great Sanhedrin in the making, he had to restate his offer. Thus, he decided to reformulate it as a binding declaration.

Such was the origin of the letter which Napoleon addressed to Champagny from Poznan on November 29, 1806:

Monsieur Champagny...

Regarding the project of the organization of the Jewish nation, it is necessary that the Sanhedrin be assembled. Call it for such a time that I can send to it all that has to be regulated.

It is necessary to remove from the Laws of Moses all that is intolerant, to declare a portion of these laws as civil and political laws and to leave of the religious laws only what is related to the moral obligations of French citizens.

Notes relating to the Sanhedrin.

1. In order to proceed in a regular manner, one should begin with the declaration that the laws of Moses contain religious as well as political dispositions, that the religious dispositions are unchangeable while this does not apply to the political dispositions which are open to modifications; that only the Great Sanhedrin is able to establish this distinction; that during the whole time during which the Jews stayed in Palestine and formed a corporate nation, the political circumstances having remained the same as in the times of Moses, the Great Sanhedrin had no cause to make this distinction; that, however, since the Israelites have left their fatherland, no Great Sanhedrin has convened.[52]

The quoted initial passages reveal the historical purpose which Napoleon ascribed to the Sanhedrin. An expression never used before appears and brings his intentions into focus: "the organization of the Jewish nation." The term covered a program, a national program for the whole Diaspora. Once again he was about to apply "one of his grandest ideas" — *l'agglomération* — to the Jewish people. While in 1799 he had failed to realize it by restoration, the formula suitable for the same aim seemed to be in 1806: *"l'organisation."* The term meant ingathering and unification, but also, by its link with the Great Sanhedrin, renascence and regeneration. A new unified law was to be created.

23

THE SESSION AND DECISION OF THE
GREAT SANHEDRIN

The proclamation of the Assembly had fixed the opening
of the Sanhedrin for October 20, 1806, but the outbreak
of war caused a considerable delay. The Great Sanhedrin
of Paris was solenmly inaugurated only on February 4, 1807.
According to the instructions, the president (*nasi*) and two
assessors were to be appointed by the Minister of the Interior. Champagny chose Sinzheim as president, Segre as
the first assessor (*av bet din*) and Abraham de Cologna as
the second assessor (*hakham*). As in the ancient Sanhedrin,
the number of the members including the president were
seventy-one. A special costume consisting of a black silken
coat and a three-cornered hat as well as the wearing of a
sword were obligatory. After having met in the home of the
president, the members assembled in the synagogue. A can-
ticle composed for this occasion was sung. It drew historical
comparison between Napoleon and ancient heroes one of
whom was Cyrus. The name of the king of Persia who was
the initiator of Israel's first Restoration occurs twice in the
poem, the last time by a link with Isaiah's prophecy directly
referring to the decree of Cyrus. After the service the dele-

gates went to the Hôtel de Ville and gathered there in the
ancient chapel of St. John, from which all religious orna-
ments had been removed. The delegates were seated after
the ancient custom in a semi-circle gathered around the nasi
according to their age, the rabbis in the front row, the laymen behind them.

Sinzheim in his opening address said: "If I look around,
upon this sublime gathering, my imagination carries me over
millenia back to the times of our people's origin, and I am
possessed by a strong sentiment which you certainly share
with me." Furtado also indulged in historical memories:

> Seized by admiration and reverence for the majesty of
> religion, and gathering in my memory all the reminis-
> cences of the beautiful days of the Holy City which
> have been recorded in our annals, I recognize in you
> the lofty court which has been erected after the long
> course of centuries and revolutions in order to assist
> in the interpretation of the divine will.

The utterances testify to the great expectations roused in the
members of the Sanhedrin, but at the same time reveal their
lack of new ideas and initiatives. "The resurrection of the
dry bones of Israel" that Abraham de Cologna believed he
was witnessing was a very shadowy happening. It did not
extend beyond the framework which had been designed by
Napoleon. Little was done to transform the creation of Napoleon into a spontaneous epoch-making event of Jewish history. It is true that the agenda of the Sanhedrin was, from
the very outset, restricted to a special task, but the first universal congress of the Jewish people offered an extraordinary

chance to raise the basic questions of Israel's existence on a worldwide forum. The members of the Sanhedrin wasted that opportunity. The Sanhedrin failed to address the Jews in countries where they still suffered under discriminatory laws. No protest was raised against the humiliating exclusion of Jews from various professions in many lands. The fact that the Emperor, at the time when the Sanhedrin convened, had entered the territory of the then largest Jewish settlement did not prompt the Sanhedrin to send an encouraging message to the Jews of Poland and Russia. No call was uttered for the creation of an effective world organization of Jews, for the revival of Hebrew, for a reform of education. In fact, the Sanhedrin showed no sign of any intention to implement Napoleon's grand idea of organizing the Jewish nation.

The Sanhedrin made haste to declare, in the *"Préamble"* to the *Décisions doctrinaires du Grand Sanhedrin* that the people of Israel does *not* form a corporate nation any more thus drawing an emphatic conclusion from Napoleon's statement that during the time when the Jews had formed a corporate nation, the Great Sanhedrin had had no cause to make a distinction between the religious and political dispositions of the laws of Moses. The writers of the *"Préamble"* were indeed most anxious to avoid the term "nation" as well as the word "Jews" altogether. Whereas they used the expression "people" only once by referring to ancient Israel, they preferred to call the Jews "descendants of Jacob," "brethren," and "correligionists." Thus, instead of becoming an exponent of Napoleon's plan to "organize the Jewish nation," the Sanhedrin officially inaugurated the practice of the Emancipation era to make Israel appear as a religious community, or even a compound of various nationally differentiated communities, rather than as one people.

The *Décisions* themselves, which followed the "Préamble," showed no significant deviation from the answers of the Assembly to the Twelve Questions. The manifesto of the Sanhedrin as a whole recognised for the first time principles which in the long run became dominant for the relation of the Diaspora to the surrounding non-Jewish world. It would nevertheless be incorrect to ignore some revivalist elements which were hidden in the manifesto. The reappearance of the Sanhedrin, "famous in our annals... after fifteen centuries," was solemnly declared and, by this token, the continuity of Jewish history emphatically recognized. Even though the identification with the ancient legislative body of Israel was highly questionable, the gathered rabbis and laymen had safeguarded the claim of the Jewish people to autonomy. And though their competence "to create religious ordinances" was open to debate, they were justified to claim the authority of cooperating in the moral regeneration of the Jewish people. There was indeed a call for a "regeneration of Israel." Even if restricted to a moral improvement, this appeal sounded like a clarion call of a new era in the history of the Jewish people.

24

THE LEGEND OF THE GREAT SANHEDRIN

The sudden dissolution of the Great Sanhedrin added much to the mystery which, from the outset, had surrounded the convocation of the body. The consternation over the premature closing of the Sanhedrin gave birth to a legend, recorded in the memoirs of Jean-Antoine Chaptal.[53] According to Chaptal, a conversation which allegedly took place between Napoleon and his uncle Joseph Fesch, the Cardinal and Archbishop of Lyons, prompted the Emperor to terminate the Sanhedrin. "Do you want indeed to bring about the end of the world?" Fesch is said to have asked Napoleon. The Archibishop explained: "Do you not know that the Holy Scriptures predict the end of the world for the moment when the Jews will be recognized as a corporate nation?" Thereupon, according to Chaptal's record, Napoleon issued the order to close the Sanhedrin.

The story, which found its way into various biographical acounts, has to be dismissed as apocryphal. Chaptal's story is nevertheless an interesting source for the reconstruction of the circumstances which might have led to the sudden dissolution of the Sanhedrin. The story reflected the hostility which the convocation of the Great Sanhedrin met in certain

Catholic circles. A. J. B. Simonini, who described himself as a military officer, addressed a letter to the famous Jesuit Barruel on August 1, 1806, in which he tried to prove that "the Judaic sect, a most formidable power owing to its enormous riches, is about to nullify Christendom." Barruel found this prototype of the ill-famed "Protocols of the Elders of Zion" worthy to be forwarded to the Pope. Pius VII approved the anti-Jewish accusations and advised him to pass the document to Fesch "in order that he may make use of it before the Emperor according to his own judgment." The recommendation of the Pope may have influenced Napoleon's decision. The tension between Napoleon and Pius VII, caused by the opposition of the Pope to Continental Blockade, was still strong. A concession to the Pope could at that stage appear profitable.

The importance of Chaptal's report consists in the revelation that the belief in the epoch-making or rather eschatological, significance of the Great Sanhedrin was current in contemporary public opinion. The exponents of these views were convinced that the purpose of the Sanhedrin was pregnant with Messianic meaning. The word that Napoleon aspired to become the "Messiah of the Jews" — so often and openly heard in the year 1799 — reappeared on the lips of many. An anonymous pamphlet entitled *"Qu'est-ce qu'un Israélite chrétien?"* maintained, on the ground of a passage from Isaiah, that Napoleon was "the Lord's Anointed who will save Israel."[54] The pamphlet was suppressed by the police (and thus saved from oblivion). A further contribution to the public debate which the Great Sanhedrin called forth was an essay published in 1808 in the Hamburg magazine

Minerva under the title *"Der Messias der Juden"* (The Messiah of the Jews). The author — named Russwurm, did not allude to the Sanhedrin or to Napoleon; he put before the Jews a decisive question on whose proper answer the granting of civil equality was dependent: "Do the Jews expect a political Messiah or do they hope for the coming of one who, without a political aim, should pursue only their ennoblement and moral improvement?"

In Austria, Napoleon's actions raised deep apprehension. The Consul in Paris, Metternich, in a letter to Count Stadion, the Foreign Minister, of September 24, 1806, gave his opinion that all the Jews look upon Napoleon as their "Messiah." Another letter of Metternich to Stadion, written on October 23, 1806, shortly after the issue of the proclamation about the convocation of the Great Sanhedrin (when Prussia was already crushed by the battles of Jena and Auerstadt) brought Napoleon's policy concerning the Jews in the perspective of his military operations: Napoleon is aspiring to become the Messiah of the vast Jewish population of Poland, just as he wants to be the liberator of the Poles. Metternich added the stern warning that unless the other governments undertake united counter-measures, the French government will succeed in attaching millions of subjects, who already feel estranged from their rulers, to its revolutionary interests.[55]

Metternich's letters were alarming. Baron de Summerau, the head of the Austrian police, submitted — on October 21, 1806— to Emperor Francis I the equally disturbing report that an invitation of the Jewish Assembly to the European Jews had been issued in which "a total regeneration of the

Jewish people" had been suggested. An invitation had actually arrived in Vienna, addressed to Bernhard Edler von Eskeles, one of the leading Jewish financiers in Austria. The Emperor immediately ordered an inquiry among the Jews about their attitudes to the Sanhedrin. He also issued an order that all necessary precautions be taken to prevent Jews of the Empire from going to Paris and assisting the Sanhedrin in any manner.

Reports from all parts of the empire soon arrived and proved that most Jews did *not* look upon Napoleon as a Messiah. Orthodox Jews exhibited an outspoken hostile attitude to the Sanhedrin, an assembly consisting of radicals. The police reported that, according to views current among Jews in Moravia, the Sanhedrin was the work of the Frankists who have numerous followers in Italy, especially in Turin, and are in contact with the daughter of Jacob Frank. This sect, the report went on, had succeeded in gaining the support of the French government which welcomed this opportunity of exerting an influence on Jewry. France has favored the numerous adherents of this sect, and from among them the delegates of the Jewish Assembly were chosen.

The most astonishing item was a summary of opinions circulating among some Moravian Jews:

> The French Government would request, secure and (if necessary) take from the Turkish Empire the city of Jerusalem with the surrounding territory and there re-establish and restore the settlement of the people of Israel. France intends to attract to this city and territory the most distinguished, wealthiest and most in-

dustrious Jews of the whole world under the promise of the protection of their religion and to direct by their speculations and enterprises the far remote southern and Egyptian colonial commerce through that place.[56]

A most venomous attack on the Sanhedrin came, however, from Russia. The Holy Synod of Moscow detested the blasphemous Jewish congress and issued an open manifesto against the Sanhedrin even before it met. The proclamation dated December 1806, declared:

> In order to bring about a debasement of the Church he [Napoleon] has convened to Paris the Jewish synagogues, restored the dignity of the rabbis and founded a new Hebrew Sanhedrin, the same infamous tribunal which once dared to condemn our Lord and Saviour Jesus Christ to the cross. And now he has the impudence to contemplate the unification of the Jews whom God in His wrath has dispersed over the surface of the earth and to organize all of them for the destruction of the Church of Christ to the purpose — oh, unspeakable audacity surpassing all the misdeeds! — that they may proclaim the Messiah in the person of Napoleon.

The same perspective also dominates a report of F. Schweitzer, a Russian official of Lublin, addressed to Czar Alexander I, dated October 19, 1806. Schweitzer was convinced that the equal rights which Napoleon had granted might estrange the Jewish population from the rulers of countries which exposed them to legal disabilities, and that this was Napoleon's real aim. In order to counteract the danger involved in this pro-Jewish policy, Schweitzer suggested the creation of a large settlement between the Don and Dnieper where the Jews would enjoy autonomy. Thus, a territorialist project was devised for the purpose of luring away the Jews of Russia from Napoleon's organization of the Jewish nation. These suspicions were completely unfounded; no trace of the Assembly or of the Sanhedrin penetrated the tightly organized and secluded world of the Jewish communities of Eastern Europe. The influence of Napoleon's campaign against Russia and march on Moscow is also difficult to evaluate because he left an imprint in legend, folktale and popular sayings rather than as a historical figure. Thus, the leaders of Hasidism are depicted in folk tales as either opposing Napoleon or furthering his cause — but not in a realistic scheme of affairs. In proverbs Napoleon appeared as a figure representing effective power and cleverness.[57]

Shortly after the dissolution of the Sanhedrin, an English translation of the French documentary report on the sessions of the Sanhedrin, which had been published in Paris by Diogene Tama, was arranged and edited by F. D. Kirwan in London. In his preface to this edition, Kirwan expressly stated that "Napoleon's gigantic mind entertains the idea of reestablishing the Jews in Palestine, and this forms a part of his plan respecting Egypt which he is well-known never to have abandoned." This conviction is openly expressed by James Bichene in a new edition of his book about the Restoration of the Jews, published in 1807. Bichene believed that the Sanhedrin constituted a link in the chain of events which was to bring about the restoration of the Jewish commonwealth in Palestine. He not only reprinted the full text of the *"Letter to the Brethren,"* but also prefaced it with the remark that "the letter was published at the suggestion of those then in power in France." A new spokesman of the British Restoration Movement, George Stanley Faber, refused to regard "the individual Bonaparte" as Antichrist: he predicted a conflagration between an "Antichristian Confederacy" headed by France and a Protestant maritime Power, both of which will attempt to restore the Jews, but only the former in an "unconverted state."

> The confederacy will successfully invade Palestine by land, will occupy Egypt, will return and attack Jerusalem and will plant the curtains of their pavillons between the seas in the glorious holy mountains... Their triumph, however, after this last exploit will be short. Assembling themselves altogether at Megiddo, they will suddenly be overthrown by the Divine word of God... so that the bulk of this mighty northern army shall miserably come to its end...

No records of official or public English reactions to the convocation of the Sanhedrin have been recorded. Nevertheless, the testimony of one most reliable witness seems to make up for this deficiency. He was Captain Thomas Ussher who brought Napoleon to Elba after his abdication in 1814. Among the subjects which he discussed with the Emperor during the voyage was also Napoleon's intention to "rebuild Jerusalem." "It was generally thought in England," Ussher declared, that the Emperor intended to do this and "that which gave rise to the supposition was the convoking of the Sanhedrin of the Jews in Paris."[58]

An historic echo to the convocation of the Great Sanhedrin was sounded by one of the most outstanding Jews of that period: Gershom Mendes Seixas, first minister of the oldest North-American congregation, Sheerith Israel, in New York. Seixas, who may well be considered the earliest American forerunner of Zionism, recognized Bonaparte's role in the realization of Israel's Messianic hopes at the time of the Eastern Expedition. He was the only contemporary Rabbi who commented upon this event and welcomed it as "the birth-pangs" of the Messianic redemption in a sermon, delivered and published in 1798. Sermons delivered between 1801 and 1804, although again referring to Israel's restoration, reflected the disappointment which the failure of Bonaparte's oriental plans had caused him.

The dimmed hopes of Seixas were rekindled by the Jewish Assembly, on January 11, 1807. He delivered a Charity Sermon in the synagogue:

> Among the many events, predicted by the Prophets, to take place, previous to the restoration of Israel to their former glory and pre-eminence, the convention of our brethren in Zarephath [France] may be viewed as one of not the least extraordinary, for under the auspices of the most powerful potentate of Europe, and after the lapse of 17 centuries since our captivity, he has collected the most learned of our Rabbonim who reside in his dominion, and invited every one, who incline to attend from other countries, to assemble in his metropolis, to form a Sanhedrin. For what purpose, or what their business will be, we cannot pretend to

say. Many things are conjectured, but none to be depended on, from what motives they were convened, we have no more knowledge of, than what is published to the whole world. At present everything appears in a favorable train, but no one can say with precision, how it will terminate.

Let us pray that the God of Israel may so direct them, that they may not be involved in difficulty and may be able to avert every possible evil. That they may find favor in the sight of their Emperor, and that he under the influence of divine grace may be a means to accomplish our re-establishment if not as a nation in our former territory, let it only be as a particular society, with equal rights and privileges of all other religious societies. This circumstance alone calls forth our gratitude to God, for His benignity, in having preserved us a distinct body, among all nations...[59]

25

A GLOOMY EPILOGUE

While the Jews were suspected of looking upon Napoleon as their Messiah and the legend of the Great Sanhedrin was giving rise to eccentric expectations outside of France, Napoleon was about to reverse the favorable trend of his policy concerning the Jews, as manifested in the convocation of the Jewish Assembly and of the Great Sanhedrin. The issue of the so called "infamous decree" of March 17, 1808, has indeed puzzled historians and, in the eyes of many, discredited the bold initiative Napoleon had taken in the Jewish cause. The dissolution of the Sanhedrin was the opening scene for a surprising turn of events. It was followed by a short closing session of the Jewish Notables who resumed their activities on March 25. For in relation to the Jewish Assembly, the Great Sanhedrin had been only an interlude. The Assembly had, it is true, completed its main work prior to the convening of the Sanhedrin. Besides answering the twelve questions, the Notables had approved the organization of French Jewry. It provided the creation of consistories, consisting of rabbis and laymen, in every department of the French empire or in every group of departments where there were at least two thousand Jews, and of a Central Consistory in Paris.

171

The question of the attitude of the state to the accusations of usury levelled against Jews remained to be solved. Pasquier and Portalis, Jr., sincerely impressed by the performance and the decisions of the Sanhedrin, supported the demands of the Jews, while Molé, advocated an exceptional legislation against them. In the State Council Portalis, Sr., the Minister of Cults, insisted upon a particular law against the Jewish population which he continued to consider a nation, utterly ignoring the protestation of the Notables that they were Frenchmen. It was the first and one of the most drastic examples during the emancipation era of the futility of any self-denial of Jewish nationhood.

Even before the State Council had concluded its deliberations the Emperor extended the delay, which by the decree of May 30, 1806, suspended the enforcing of Jewish claims. This severe measure greatly disturbed French Jewry; it was correctly recognized as a foreboding of things to come. Alarmed by such a prospect, Furtado made up his mind to intervene with the Emperor in order to avert the danger. In June, 1807, he embarked, accompanied by Maurice Levy of Nancy, on a journey to Poland. Napoleon had just won the decisive victory over the Russians at Friedland (June 14) and had taken up residence at Tilsit on the Njemen. There for the first time a representative of Jewry was received by the Emperor, who promised that the rights of the Jews would not be impaired.

The definite proposals of the State Council were submitted to the Emperor on February 29, 1808. On March 17, Napoleon signed the two imperial decrees concerning the Jews of France. The introduction of the consistorial organization was combined with restrictive measures of most damaging, though temporary character. The decree about the formation, the rights and duties of the consistories and of the Central Consistory was based on the proposal which had been approved by the Jewish Assembly. It created a constitution of French Jewry providing the guarantee and safeguard of Jewish worship. Although marred by the imposition of tasks which served the benefit of the government alone, the consistorial organization was an innovation of epoch-making significance. It abolished the traditional autonomous communities, and transformed them into one coherent body. Moreover, the Central Consistory emerged from the Jewish Assembly as a new, permanent, unifying Jewish authority.

The accompanying decree replaced the suspension of the execution of debts to Jews by more draconian measures. The debts due to Jewish creditors were in many cases declared simply void or open to reduction or suspended by the courts. The measure almost meant an annulment of monetary obligations. No Jew was permitted to engage in trade without special permission of the municipality. No Jewish conscript was allowed to offer a substitute for himself, though non-Jews enjoyed this privilege. The restrictive measures were to be in force for ten years. The issue of the decree was a major disaster not only because of the economic consequences but, on account of the moral effects which the humiliation of emancipated French Jewry caused inside and outside the Jewish world. The injury fell even more heavily with regard to the exalted hopes the Jewish Assembly and the Great Sanhedrin had awakened.

26

IN THE FOOTSTEPS OF SOLOMON OR HEROD

The memoirs Napoleon dictated on St. Helena are not always a reliable historical source, but the information given by Napoleon to Dr. O'Meara, his faithful Irish physician, in reply to O'Meara's inquiry into Napoleon's reasons "for having encouraged the Jews so much," are very elucidating:

> I wanted to make them leave off usury, and become like other men. There were a great many Jews in the countries I reigned over; by removing their disabilities, and by putting them upon an equality with Catholics, Protestants, and others, I hoped to make them to become good citizens, and conduct themselves like the rest of the community. I believe that I should have succeeded in the end. My reasoning with them was, that as their rabbis explained to them that they ought not practise usury against their own tribes, but were allowed to practise it with Christians and others, that, therefore, as I had restored them to all their privileges, and made them equal to my other subjects, they must consider me like Solomon or Herod, to be the head of their nation, and my subjects as brethren of a tribe

174

similar to theirs. Consequently, they were not permitted to deal usuriously with them or me, but to treat us as if we were of the tribe of Judah. Enjoying similar privileges to my subjects, they were, in like manner, to pay taxes, and submit to the laws of conscription, and to other laws. By this I gained many soldiers. Besides, I should have drawn great wealth to France, as the Jews were very numerous and would have flocked to a country where they enjoyed such privileges. Moreover, I wanted to establish a universal liberty of conscience and thought to make all men equal, whether Protestants, Catholics, Mohammedans, Deists, or others; so that their religion should have no influence in getting them employment under government. In fact, that it should neither be the means of serving, nor of injuring them: and that no objection should be made to a man's getting a situation on the score of religion, provided he were fit for it in other respects. I made everything independent of religion.[60]

It goes without saying that Napoleon's recognition of Jewish nationhood here was strictly opposed to the declarations of the Jewish Assembly and of the Great Sanhedrin that the Jews have actually — in France — become Frenchmen. In blatant contradiction to the answers of the Notables and of the Sanhedrin, Napoleon repeated the charge against the rabbis of having sanctioned the practice of usury as far as non-Jews were concerned. Thus, Napoleon's answer to O'Meara reflects the basic ideas which he held about the Jews before the convocation of the Notables. It was a blend of his genuine belief in the perpetuation of the Jewish nation and of the conviction which, since it had been implanted in him by de Bonald, had become an *idée fixe*: that the Jews were inclined to usury by virtue of a religious ordinance. Two other ideas, each of which he had adopted only at a later stage, were linked with this aspect of the Jewish people. During the deliberations which preceded the issue of the decree of May 30, 1806 he made the resolution to "correct" the Jews; the time when he conceived the plan to summon the Great Sanhedrin probably also gave birth to the idea which for the first and only time is recorded in the answer to O'Meara: to become recognized as the head of dispersed nation, like Solomon or Herod. The emergence of this vision was undoubtedly connected with the intention of organizing the Jewish nation within the Diaspora, but the name of Solomon clearly pointed to the roots which the idea had in the first stage of Napoleon's interest in the solution of the Jewish question. The city of Solomon had been his first thought on the eve of his thrust into the Holy Land. The figure of the builder of the Temple rose again before his eyes when he was about to transform Paris into a New Jerusalem. He realized that to have the Emperor of the French recognized as another son of David was far more problematical than his identification with Charlemagne. It is indeed a sign of the political reality he ascribed to his aspiration of becoming the head of the Jewish nation that he visualized himself at the second thought rather as a counterpart of Solomon's successor of non-Jewish origin — the Idumean Herod the Great. Thus, the dramatic reference to the famous kings of Israel proves that he dreamed of indeed becoming, if not, as many suspected, a "Messiah" of the Jews, then at least a Messianic ruler of the dispersed Jewish nation who would unite *l'universalité des Israélites* and bring about their moral regeneration. This aspiration may also explain why no mention of the Jewish Assembly or of the Great Sanhedrin is to be found in Napoleon's answer to O'Meara, though the latter apparently alluded to these extraordinary gatherings — so well remembered in Great Britain — when he in his question referred to the encouragement the Jews had received from the Emperor. The intended transformation of the Jewish nation was presented as Napoleon's own work, based on his own vision and idea. The creator of the Code was not prepared to share with anybody else the glory of having given a new law and a new status to the Jewish nation.

PART SEVEN

AFTERMATH OF THE NAPOLEONIC ERA

27

THE IMPACT OF NAPOLEON ON THE JEWS OF THE EMANCIPATION ERA

Napoleon's downfall, though hailed all over Europe as the liberation from tyranny, was followed almost everywhere by political reaction. No nation was as hard hit by this upheaval as the Jewish people. In Italy and Holland, in Germany and, to some extent, in Poland, the Jews had enjoyed for the first time, equal rights; they had played their part in public life and distinguished themselves in various fields. This first emancipation period became, through the collapse of the French Empire, a short intermezzo of less than a decade in Jewish history. The Jews of France retained their civil rights and their constitution (though the "Infamous decree" remained in force in the Alsace Departments until 1818). The Jews of the Netherlands preserved their equality and became the beneficiary of the first international guarantee, granted to the reestablished state of the Netherlands by the allied Powers. The status of the Jews became an issue at the Congress of Vienna (1814-15) and thus, for the first time, "the Jewish Question" was made an object of international politics. This must be considered a consequence of the public discussions of the Jewish Assembly and of the Great Sanhedrin.

The worst setback was inflicted upon the Jews of the Papal States. It would almost seem as if Pius VII had taken revenge on the Jewish population of his territory for the humiliation which he had suffered. He was not content with their confinement behind the walls of the reerected ghetto, but obliged the Jews to wear the yellow badge and to attend conversionist sermons. In the Kingdom of Sardinia the Jews were thrown back into the ghetto and not allowed to build synagogues. The Austrians in northern Italy excluded the Jews of Lombardy and Venetia, like those of other Austrian provinces, from public offices and — with some exceptions — from the ownership of real estate. In Frankfurt the franchise for which the Jews had paid 440,000 gulden in 1811 was revoked on January 16, 1814, while Luebeck and Bremen expelled the Jews who had settled there under French occupation. In Prussia semi-medieval conditions were created for the Jews in the eastern provinces, and Jewish rights, promised in 1812, were not carried out or annulled. Amidst the new reaction Jews felt strengthened by the memories of Napoleon, who became the symbol of liberation for the coming Jewish generations. Jews, liberated from the ghetto and raised to equal citizenship with German gentiles continued to regret the downfall of Napoleon their liberator. Even though, in the 1813 "War of Liberation," many German and Austrian Jews sided with their countrymen against the "despot," what they defended was *his* work, the rights which they had obtained or hoped to obtain from their governments according to the principles he had proclaimed Had the Sanhedrin of Paris, after all, not obliged the Jews to defend their homelands where they enjoyed civil equality? The disappointment caused after the defeat of Napoleon, which they had helped to bring about, made the Napoleonic era appear to them as a "Paradise Lost." Thus, the legend of Napoleon took new roots among the Jews.

In 1852, only four years before his death, Heinrich Heine, lying in his "mattress-grave" in Paris, said to an English publicist, who presented him with a copy of the English literary journal *The Critic* containing a translation of Heine's poem *"Die beiden Grenadiere"* (The Two Grenadiers), words which might well be termed his Confession Napoleonica:

> Ah *"Nach Frankreich zagen zwei Grenadiere..."* Almost the first poem I ever wrote — *"The Grenadiers!"* It was in 1814 that I composed it; I was fifteen then; I remember singing it low to myself one evening early in summer, on the bank of the Rhine, just when the news had come that the Emperor was to be exiled to Elba. My friend! I have gone through every phase of modern thought and feeling — I have been Werther, Rene, Lara, Faust, Mephistopheles — I have risen into a self-deification with that prince of cloud-embracers, Hegel — I have plunged into the dreamy abyss of mystical ecstasy. I have dined with the literature of despair, I have helped to chant the frantic psalm Young Germany — I have earned a right to be called the Corphaeus of sensualism — I have sped through the universe and veiled it in a soft mist of irony — but I have never swerved from my faith in the Emperor. I have never ceased to doubt his advent — My Emperor — the ruler of the people for the people.

He described the overwhelming sight he got of the Emperor as a young boy when the latter rode through Dusseldorf, and he took delight in memories of Napoleon's glory on the battlefield of Marengo. In reviewing Walter Scott's *The Life of Napoleon Buonaparte,* he pitied the poet who fortefeited his laurels by misrepresenting the Emperor. He called St. Helena the "tomb to which the peoples of the Orient and Occident pilgrimage in multicolored ships in order to strengthen their hearts by the memories of the deeds of the secular savior who suffered under Hudson Lowe as it is written in the gospels of Las Casse, O'Meara and Automoarchim." Critical passages, however, can also be found in Heine's work: "My homage is not to the actions but to the genius of the man, I love him unconditionally only up to the eighteenth Brumaire." This distinction between the consummator of the Great Revolution and the destroyer of the Republic occurs again and again. A passage in his *Französische Zustände* ("French Affairs") refers to the picture of the Emperor visiting the hospital at Jaffa or lying on his death bed at St. Helena which he found most frequently in peasant homes in Normandy; Napoleon resembling a Savior who cures the afflicted by a touch and dying the death of expiation. Heine, however, disagreed with this interpretation of the pictures: "We who have adopted a different symbolism see in the martyrdom of Napoleon at St. Helena no expiation in the sense here indicated, for the Emperor there did penance for his most fatal error, for his faithlessness to his mother, the Revolution."

Nevertheless, sincere admiration remained the dominant note of Heine's attitude to Napoleon. He saw in him the

"Moses of the French who like the latter has led the people through the desert in order to cure them." He called him "the only great ruler, the only kingly hero to whom France could give her heart." He recognized him as "the new man, the man in whom this new age mirrors itself so gloriously that we are well-nigh dazzled thereby, and never think meanwhile of the vanished past nor of the faded splendor."

Heine was fully aware of the decisive significance of Napoleon's rule for the Jews: "My becoming a Christian is the fault of those Saxons who suddenly changed saddles at Leipzig, or of Napoleon, who really did not have to go to Russia, or of the teacher of geography at Brienne, who did not tell him that Moscow winters are very cold." Bitter irony covers the historical fact that Napoleon's defeat stopped Emancipation and plunged Jewish youth into utter disillusionment and despair. "Emancipation, not only of the Irish, Greeks, Jews of Frankfort, West-Indian negroes and similar oppressed peoples, emancipation of the whole world, above all of Europe" seemed to Heine to be the meaning of the wars Napoleon had fought against the rulers of Europe. Whatever Heine's share in the universal appreciation of Napoleon, the Jewish legend of Napoleon was to a great extent his work. It was very much due to Heine that Napoleon the Emancipator, the unifier of Europe, more than any other vision of the Corsican, seized the imagination of generations of Jews.[61]

It would be, erroneous, however, to assume that admiration of Napoleon was generally accepted by the Jewish world. Ludwig Börne, the famous publicist, differed sharply from Heine in his views of Napoleon. While Heine, though critical of Napoleon's imperial policy, recognized the merits of Napoleon the Emperor, Börne made a clear-cut distinction between the two periods: "Bonaparte was great, noble, magnanimous, he fought for Liberty and Justice; but Napoleon was imperious, arbitrary, evil and fraudulent." This judgment was to become part and parcel of another, anti-Napoleonic, legend which went through many stages in the course of the nineteenth century until it culminated in Leo Tolstoy's *War and Peace.* Jews had a considerable share in this development as well. The leading role they took in the rise of socialism and pacifism, of sociology and psychology made them participate in the shattering of hero-worship, above all of Napoleon cult. Moreover, students of Jewish history often felt prejudiced against Napoleon on account of his latter "infamous" legislative acts. At the same time the ideas of Enlightenment lost much of their attraction for those who searched for the Jewish values. Napoleon himself, with his lack of understanding for Jewish tradition, seemed a hostile force rather than a patron of the Jewish people. The French Jewish author Jean-Richard Bloch, warned the Jews of the danger of following Napoleon's example. Napoleon represented the "loss of balance between the frenzy of individualism and the capacity of social humanity to include frenzies and individuals." In the extreme contrast, the Jews are, according to Bloch, "fanatics for universal happiness, justice on earth, the future of society."[62]

28

THE INFLUENCE ON THE RISE OF ZIONISM

The impetus given to the British Movement for the Restoration of the Jews by Bonaparte's Oriental Expedition, by his Proclamation and by the convocation of the Great Sanhedrin continued to be felt in the first decades of the nineteenth century. The Restoration seemed to have come within perceptible distance. All that remained doubtful was its exact date and the manner of its realization. George Stanley Faber published a second amplified edition of his work as a postscript to the Napoleonic epoch between 1814 and 1818. Besides Faber, new supporters of the movement appeared like John Fry, author of the much discussed book, *The Second Advent,* the forceful Scottish preacher, Edward Irving, and the noted writer William Cunninghame, whose *Letters and Studies* contained a study about *"The Literal Restoration of Israel to Their Own Land."* In 1815 — the year which terminated the Napoleonic era — Lord Byron, Napoleon's fervent admirer, published his great *"Hebrew Melodies",* the songs of Israel's steadfast faith, its grief for the lost country, its sorrows over the desolation of the sacred land and the people's homelessness.

The increased intensity of the voices heard in England immediately after Napoleon's downfall calling for the Restoration of the Jews, and an unprecedented activity of its advocates towards the realization of that aim provide evidence of the strong influence of Napoleon on British sympathizers with the idea of Israel's rebirth. The example of Napoleon's own efforts on behalf of the Jewish people and the magic of his personality as well as the negative effects of his eclipse — the political reaction and the outburst of anti-Jewish riots in Germany in 1819 — worked in the same direction. *"A Call of the Christians and the Hebrews"* was the title of a pamphlet published in 1818 by an unknown writer under the pseudonym Theaetetus. The author envisaged the reestablishment of the Jews in the Holy Land by peaceful cooperation of Christians and Jews. His enthusiastic appeal to Britain, "the maritime people," to "assume the glorious enterprise" was coupled with a similar call to the Jews which was very reminiscent of the *"Letter to the Brethren"* and of the Proclamation.

The London Society for Promoting Christianity among the Jews (established in 1807) combined the evangelizing and conversionist tendency of the movement with an immediate political activity in the person of Lewis Way, millenarian and romantic, lawyer, theologian, preacher, poet and diplomat.[63] Way traveled through France, Holland, Germany, visited Russia and there studied the life of the Jews. He succeeded in arousing the interest of Czar Alexander in his scheme of establishing, in South Russia, settlements of baptized Jews. Way's pro-Jewish activities reached their climax after his return from Russia. In September, 1818, a conference of the Holy Alliance took place at Aix-la-Chapelle to discuss the settlement of European affairs. Way went to Aix and submitted a *"Mémoire sur l'Etat des Israélites,"* dated Brussels, September 28, 1818, to the Czar. The Almighty, Way declared, wills that the Jews should one day be raised to a rank higher than they ever occupied before, but not through abolition of their national distinctions. Therefore, he argued, the Jews should be granted emancipation without interfering with their particular status. Way expressed the hope that the Powers assembled at Aix might do something to bring about ultimate restoration of the Jews. Such an asembly of sovereigns, if imbued with the spirit of Cyrus, could issue an edict which would create a country in a day and cause a people to be born instantly. Alexander seemed to be well disposed to Way's proposals. He instructed his representatives, Nesselrode and Kapodistrias, to lay the "Mémoire" before the conference. But the only official record is a brief note in the minutes of the conference signed by all participants, taking notice — with a complimentary reference to the author — of the "attached printed document on the subject of a reform of civil and political legislation in regard to the Jewish people." Way's appearance in Aix-la-Chapelle represented a milestone in the history of the Restoration movement. He was the first spokesman of the movement to plead the cause of Restoration before an international forum. Above all, his ideas as expounded in the printed edition of his *"Mémoires sur l'Etat des Israélites"* are a blend of the millenarian views which formed the basis of the religious restoration doctrine and of Napoleonic political plans regarding the Jewish people.

History has also provided an astonishing Jewish American parallel to the tendency of which Lewis Way was the British embodiment. His contemporary, Mordecai Manuel Noah, the self-styled "Judge in Israel," was the counterpart of the self-appointed Christian advocate of the Jewish people.[64] Born in 1785, Noah witnessed from Philadelphia and Charleston Bonaparte's meteoric rise to power. A voracious reader — and like Napoleon, an eager student of history, — a journalist and author of historical plays he could not miss the march of the events that inaugurated the Napoleonic era. In the gigantic struggle which raged on the European continent and which spread to the Western hemisphere, Noah sided definitely with France against England. In 1812, when war fever swept the United States, we find the twenty-six-year-old Noah among the most impassioned "War Hawks." In 1811 he received an appointment as Consul for the United States at Riga, but the outbreak of the war with Russia prevented him from accepting this post. Two years later — on May 28, 1813 — Noah was on his way to Africa in order to serve there as "Consul of the United States for the city and kingdom of Tunisia." Soon after presenting his credentials Noah demonstrated his admiration of Napoleon in his official consular capacity. During the "Hundred Days," Mr. Debois de Tainville, formerly Consul at Algiers, arrived in Tunis bearing the tricolored flag, and asked the Bey of Tunis to be recognized as Consul-General of the restored Emperor. The Bey complied with this request in spite of the protest raised by the Charge d'Affaires of Louis XVIII. Nevertheless, when the white flag of the king was replaced by the tricolored flag on the French consulate, all the accredited consuls re-

fused to show the customary honor — with one single excep-
tion, The United States. There can be little doubt that Noah,
an admirer of Napoleon and a sharp critic of the Holy Alliance, welcomed the occasion of paying his respects to the
Emperor. The ceremonial visit he paid to Mr. Debois de
Tainville and the dinner to which he invited the controversial
consul was probably a rare instance of diplomatic rejoicing
at the short-lived revival of the French empire.

Several weeks later, Mordecai Manuel Noah suffered his
own Waterloo. On July 30, 1815, an American squadron
under the command of Commodore Decatur landed at Cape
Carthage. The marines were under arms and as they received
the Consul with the usual honors Decatur handed Noah a
letter from James Monroe, the Secretary of State. It informed
him that the President had deemed it expedient to revoke
his commission; the reasons given for the recall were even
more depressing. At the time of Noah's appointment, the
letter read, it was not known that the religion which he professed would form any obstacle to the exercise of his consular
functions. Recent information proved that it would produce
a very unfavorable effect. Noah's accounts, too, would re-
quire a more particular explanation. This was one of the
most significant moments in Noah's life. Monroe's letter
meant the collapse of Noah's diplomatic career. Noah was
thrown back into his private sphere — a sphere of his personal resources and of his Jewishness.

A few years later in a *Discourse Delivered at the Conse-
cration of the Synagogue Shearith Israel* in New York on
April 17, 1818, he expostulated on the seven million Jews
in the world:

...a number greater than at any period of our history, and possessing more wealth, activity, influence, and talents, than any body of people of their number on earth. The signal for breaking the Turkish scepter in Europe, will be their emancipation; they will deliver the north of Africa from its oppressors: they will assist to establish civilization in European Turkey; and may revive commerce and the arts in Greece; they will march in triumphant numbers, and possess themselves once more of Syria, and take their rank among the governments of the Earth. This is, not fancy. I have been too much among them in Europe and Africa — I am too well acquainted with their views and sentiments in Asia, to doubt their intentions. They hold the purse strings, and can wield the sword; they can bring 100,000 men into the field. Let us then hope that the day is not far distant when, from the operation of liberal and enlightened measures, we may look towards that country where our people have established a mild, just, and honorable government, accredited by the world, and admired by all good men.

The *Discourse*, which Noah delivered before the community was his debut as a Jewish leader. Two years had passed since the death of Gershom Mendes Seixes, his former teacher. Noah now stood on the pulpit from which Seixas had preached his sermon on the Great Sanhedrin of Paris in 1806. Noah's *Discourse* was intended to be a political manifesto — the first Jewish statement of a national policy since the voices called forth by Bonaparte's Eastern Expedition. It was fashioned in the spirit of the *"Letter to the Brethren,"* of the Proclamation and Aaron ben Levi's Call. Noah himself had no doubt that the *Discourse* was to be regarded in such a perspective. He sent copies of it to the living ex-Presidents of the United States and John Adams replied:

> ...I really wish the Jews again in Judea as an independent nation, for, as I believe, the most enlightened men of it have participated in the amelioration of the philosophy of the age. Once restored to an independent government, and no longer persecuted, they would soon wear away some of the asperities and peculiarities of their character.

It took another three years until Noah felt able to attempt the realization of the plan he had outlined broadly in the Letter to the Children of Israel. These were eventful years in Noah's life. In 1822 he had, after a hard struggle, won the support of Tammany Hall and soon afterwards was appointed Sheriff of New York. He was at the peak of his political career, though he considered this achievement only a temporary step. A sudden crushing setback proved to be a painful analogy of his recall from Tunis. A magnanimous act — the release of prisoners from the debtor's jail during a yellow fever epidemic — exposed him to anti-Semitic attacks. The psychological effect of this campaign provided a strong stimulus to Noah's Jewish plan: Noah's friend, Samuel Leggett, had acquired about 2,500 acres of Grand Island, N.Y., which were designated and publicized as "Ararat: City of Refuge." On September 15, 1825, in Buffalo, the "Ararat" project was inaugurated. The details have been carefully recorded; the booming of a cannon in the early morning and Noah, in a rich judicial robe of crimson silk trimmed with ermine, a medal of gold pending from his neck, leading a procession of Royal Arch Masons and Knights Templars, ascending the pulpit of St. Paul's Episcopal Church in order to deliver his address — A Jewish Declaration of Independence — employed the expression "Proclamation to the Jews"; it was a political instrument par excellence imbued with a Napoleonic spirit. Noah invited the Jews to take possession of the land in order to renew their national existence and to prepare themselves for the "great and final re-entry in their ancient heritage which the times strongly predict." Only the precedent events of the Napoleonic era could justify such a tone. In fact, it has been correctly observed that Noah, in his Proclamation, spoke in a dictatorial manner. There was only one dictator in the lifetime with whom he could identify himself.

There was, finally, a particular feature of Noah's Proclamation to the Jews which illuminates his connection with the Napoleonic era. He empowered the Consistory of Paris to choose once every four years a Judge of Israel. He authorized the same body "to name three discreet persons to visit the United States and make such report to the nation as the actual condition shall warrant," and named Abraham de Cologna, the president of the Consistory of Paris, to the first place among the commissioners whom he appointed.

Noah's proclamation to the Jews called forth more attention than its prototype of 1799. In America and Europe, the message of the new Judge in Israel was discussed in private and in the press.

Eduard Gans, a renowned Hegelian scholar of Roman law, was at first enthusiastic but his friend Heinrich Heine made fun of the idea and called it "Ganstown." The worthy Rabbis Cologna of Paris, Hershell of London and Andrade of Bordeaux refused, with biting irony, the honor of serving as Noah's commissars. The quixotic, megalomaniacal, elements of the foundation of "Ararat" where no single Jew tried to settle were obvious to any observer.

In the old world, the memory of the first attempt to restore Israel lived on, particularly among the British advocates of this aim. More than thirty years after Bonaparte's Eastern Expedition, Michael Russell, subsequently Bishop of Glasgow and Galloway, shared the hopes in a Jewish national rebirth and summed up his views in a memorable passage in his book, *Palestine, or the Holy Land: From the Earliest Period to the Present Time:*

> There is no doubt that Napoleon frequently remarked in reference to Acre, "the fate of the East is in that place". Nor was this observation made at random, for had the French subdued Djezzar and buried his army in the ruins of the fortress, the whole of Palestine and Syria would have submitted to their dominion. He expected besides a cordial reception from the Druzes, those war-like and semi-barbarous tribes who inhabit the valleys of Libanus, and who, like all the other subjects of the Ottoman Government, had felt the pressure

of the Pasha's tyranny. His eyes were likewise turned towards the Jews, who in every commotion which affects Syria are accustomed to look for indications of that happy change destined, in the eye of their faith, to restore the kingdom of Israel, in the latter days. It was not indeed till a period somewhat more recent that he openly extended his protection to the descendants of Abraham; but it is not improbable that the notion had occurred to him during his Eastern campaign, of employing them for the purpose of establishing an independent sovereignty in Palestine, devoted to his ulterior views in the countries beyond the Euphrates.

A series of events which in the thirties of the nineteenth century set the Near East in turmoil and brought Palestine within the orbit of European politics was a direct continuation of the disturbances caused by Bonaparte's campaign. The central figure of this process was Mohammed Ali, the maker of modern Egypt, born in the same year as Napoleon Bonaparte. The former Albanian tobacco dealer would never have become the founder of a new Egyptian dynasty if the landing of Bonaparte in Egypt had not led to his emergence as a Turkish war leader; after the departure of the French he crushed the power of the Mamelukes, was appointed Egyptian Viceroy, and finally broke away from Sultan Mahmud II and declared war on him. His struggle which, with intermissions, went on from 1831 to 1841, carried Egypt's boundaries to the threshold of the Turkish empire and provoked a serious crisis in Europe. The Eastern Question was born and remained for many decades to come *the* central problem of world politics.

The rise of the Eastern Question marked a new stage in the history of the Restoration movement. The war which was fought on the soil of Palestine in the year 1840-41 between Mohammed Ali and the Allied Powers — Great Britain, Prussia, Austria and Turkey — with the French, under Thiers, backing Mohammed Ali against the coalition, was a strange counterpart of the Napoleonic invasion. Once again, Acre was the main target of the invading force. The fortress which had withstood Bonaparte's onslaught for months, was taken by an attack from the sea within three days. In February, 1841, the allies entered Damascus, and Egyptian rule over Syria, of which the Holy Land was a part, came to an end.

It seemed as if a situation as propitious for the Jewish people as in 1799 had been created. The Land of Israel was in the hands of the Western Powers and its further destiny became the subject of diplomatic negotiations at the conference of London. Numerous voices demanding the restoration of the Jews were heard. The scheme of Lord Ashley (the seventh Lord Shaftesbury) for a guarantee by the Powers for the resettlement of the Jewish people on the soil of Palestine, Palmerston's note to the Porte in favor of Jewish immigration to Palestine, the appeal of Colonel Charles Henry Churchill to Moses Montefiore to organize a diplomatic representation of the Jews, are but some highlights of the British restorationist activity of those days which surpassed any previous campaign.[65]

With the ascent of Napoleon III France again became for

a short period the principal scene of the efforts to revive the Jewish nation. Joseph Salvador, physician, historian and philosopher, created in his profound work, *Paris, Rome, Jerusalem,* published in 1860, a philosophy of the fundamental changes that had taken place in the realm of world politics between 1789 and the end of the Crimean War in 1856. Salvador recognized the epoch-making role which Napoleon Bonaparte had played in making the Jewish people an important element of this momentous development. The Eastern Expedition and — most amazingly — the battle at Mount Tabor in particular, was described by Salvador as a turning point of history:

> The inaugurator of the nineteenth century leads the political genius of the French revolution. He carries the flame of modern science into the Biblical Orient, into the ancient regions of Providence, up to the very land of the Jews; he prepares there, from afar, the great question that manifested itself in the year 1840;... In this Biblical Orient, on the Mediterranean, on the shores reminding of Moses, Jesus, Mohammed, the mighty men... receives a kind of a new baptism; he makes Egypt tremble under his feet, and renders a new voice to the pyramids which had remained silent for a millenia. Moreover, the same man escaped from being submerged by the reflux of the water on the same spot of the Red Sea on which Moses so gloriously had led a whole people in order to let it pass, by divine law, from slavery to freedom. Finally, the inaugurator of the nineteenth century applies the ensigns which have been adopted by

the new freedom to the most ancient races of the Holy
Land; he carries the baner signifying the redemption
of the rights of the nations to victory and lets intonate
a fiery and terrible hymn against the tyrants on the
foot of the Mount Tabor, this means on the very place
where one of the great representatives of justice and
independence of nations, where the strong woman, Deborah, likewise had recited a song burning with a warlike and liberating spirit against the oppressors (p.
169-70)

An unequivocal advocate of Napoleon's oriental and, above
all, of his restorationist plans was Ernest Laharanne, who was
employed in the office of Emperor Napoleon III. In his pamphlet, *"La nouvelle Question d'Orient Empire d'Egypte et
d'Arabie, Reconstruction de la Nationalité Juive,"* Laharanne
appealed to France to realize these plans. Passionate exhorta-
tion of the Jews, reminiscent of the Napoleonic documents,
appears again and again. Laharanne appealed to the Jews,
who had once been a strong people, to rebuild the doors of
Jerusalem instead of the Temple, and like the author of the
"Letter to the Brethren," he expected the Jewish people, once
resettled on the spot where three worlds meet, to bring civilization to the yet unripe nations. Above all, Laharanne visualized, quite in the Napoleonic fashion, cooperation between
France and the Jews: They must march together and re-
vitalize the desolate Land of Israel. Laharanne's pamphlet
remained without immediate political effects but influenced
Moses Hess, the most outstanding Jewish precursor of Theodor Herzl. In his famous book, *Rome and Jerusalem,* (1862),

Hess frequently quotes Laharanne. Thus, the Napoleonic tradition made itself felt at the very beginning of the modern Zionist movement.

The wave of historic events set in motion by Bonaparte's invasion of Palestine continued to work through subsequent decades. There was, however, no prospect of reestablishing the Jewish commonwealth, until the course shown to the Jewish people by the *"Letter to the Brethren"* implied in the Proclamation and urged in Rabbi Aaron's letter, was taken up and pursued methodically. Exactly one century later this essential requirement of Restoration was fulfilled by Theodor Herzl. The genesis of his achievement has become a glorious chapter of Jewish history. In fact, the epic of the nine years during which the assimilated Austrian writer transformed himself into the leader of the Jewish nation and gained diplomatic recognition for the dispersed people is still an inexhaustible subject of biographers and historians. Strangely enough the analysis of this amazing metamorphosis shows that Napoleon's influence on Herzl was not the least among the factors that brought the epoch-making result.

Herzl started his political career in Paris. In October 1891, he went there as a correspondent of the Viennese journal *Neue Freie Presse.* French literature and French politics became the very atmosphere of his life. *Das Palais Bourbon* ("The Bourbon Palace"), a collection of his Paris essays was the literary product of these years. "Paris grasped me and has shaken me thoroughly," he wrote in a letter of May 19, 1895, to his friend Heinrich Teweles in Prague. "What have I not seen and experienced here! You have read about a part of it in the paper. But I cannot tell you what shocks

I have experienced daily and hourly. One becomes another man, another artist by that." It was indeed Paris of the Third Republic under the presidency of Carnot and Casimir-Périer, with its fights between the monarchists and republicans, the Paris of Alphonse Daudet and Emile Zola, of Drumont and *La Libre Parole,* the Paris of rising anti-Semitism, above all the Dreyfus Affair, that stirred up the soul and mind of Theodor Herzl, and by the same token, made him conscious of his responsibility towards the Jewish people. A great political idea had dawned on him in those days. He not only conceived this idea but a certainty was born in him that he was called to transform it into reality:

> I have been pounding away for some time at a work of tremendous magnitude. I don't know even now if I will be able to carry it through. It bears the aspect of a mighty dream. For days and weeks it has saturated me to the limits of my consciousness; it goes with me everywhere, hovers behind my ordinary talk, peers at me over the shoulders of my funny little journalistic work, overwhelms and intoxicates me.[66]

He had "become another man, another artist." While he still hesitated to use the proper name for this new man, he felt in his innermost heart that he had become the invisible leader of the Jewish people.

There was among Herzl's contemporaries one man on whom his attention was focused in those early days. Bismarck, the unifier of the German nation and founder of the new German empire, stood in the foreground of Herzl's personal and political interests. In his eightieth year, Bismarck appeared to Herzl as the embodiment of creative statesmanship. One figure, however, loomed behind him, towering over the "iron chancellor," for the image of Napoleon I still dominated the public scene. It was, above all, omnipresent in Paris. Herzl met it everywhere, on the Place Vendôme and under the Arch of Triumph, in the magnificent buildings gathered around the *Invalides* where the remains of the Emperor surrounded by the flags captured in his battles commanded holy reverence.

Napoleon was also the subject of an avalanche of publications. The memoirs of Pasquier, Chaptal, Talleyrand and Roederer; biographies of the Emperor by Frederick Masson, Arthur Levy and others, as well as many novels, poems and dramas.

Theodor Herzl, the journalist, playwright and statesman in-the-making was most susceptible to this atmosphere. He perceived the overwhelming contrast between the Corsican and the contemporary masters of France. Herzl was attracted by the great emancipator, the organizer and legislator of Europe. In fact, although he hardly dared to confess it to himself, he discovered in the character of the immortal Emperor, the dreamer and doer, a strong affinity with his own.

In a feuilleton published in the *Neue Freie Presse* on January 11, 1894. Herzl dealt with the newest fashion of the Paris boulevard: Napoleonism. "There is nothing more new than Napoleon I. Truly, he is not yet dead. Every night he leaves his tomb under the dome of the *Invalides* and talks from all possible stages to the wonderful and variable people of France," Herzl described a play, *Napoleon*, by Laya, which was actually a biographical *revue* in 5 tableaux. Al-

though very critical of the literary qualities of the play, Herzl
dwelt on two scenes which impressed him very strongly:

> Before the battle of Austerlitz the Guard is marching
> before the Emperor. The songs of the soldiers mix with
> the sounds of the brass and the drums. The flag ap-
> pears. In this moment the Emperor respectfully un-
> covers his head before the tricolor fastened under the
> golden eagle. The flag salute is in France always a
> moving event, for this people has the religion of the
> flag. But how does it appear when some civil president
> lifts his well-pressed high hat, and how differently when
> the Emperor does it... Napoleon performs by this ges-
> ture an act of such a symbolic greatness, as the flag
> itself stands for. The soldiers cannot help recognizing
> in this pierced rag on the pole a miraculous sign. The
> flag becomes a mystical thing. Napoleon added to this
> heritage of the Revolution, the tricolor, his splendid
> eagle and now he bows before his own military sym-
> bol... Does he stand before the flag with a real emotion
> or is he also here the "actor"? True is at any case his
> contribution on the Berezina. This is another picture
> which arrests. A landscape covered with snow, and the
> retreat is in progress. The brave men are freezing. Even
> those who are yet standing upright, do not want to
> proceed... Lie down and be covered by the snow! In
> this moment one of the Marshals advised the Emperor
> to employ the ultimate means to cheer up the tired
> men: to let play and sing the Marseillaise.
> The old revolutionary song? The Emperor hesitates,

but then he yet gives the order. Yes, now the soldiers are moving in a better mood. But the Emperor stands there broken, and when the unhappy flag is waving along, he again uncovers his head. The snow falls and covers his head and shoulders, but the Emperor hardly notices it.

The deed by which Herzl definitely entered the realm of politics was his visit to Baron Maurice de Hirsch. At the end of May, 1895, he had written to Hirsch a letter requesting "a Jewish — political conversation, which perhaps will have its effect when you and I will no longer be here." Hirsch's invitation followed, and the meeting took place in the palace of the Baron on June 2. For the first time Herzl revealed his revolutionary plan. The principal question he raised was, however, related neither to anti-Semitism nor to the Jewish state:

> During our two thousand years of dispersion we have been without united political leadership. I hold this to be our chief misfortune. It has done us more harm than all the persecutions. It has rotted and ruined us from within. There has been no one — even out of the selfish ambition to be our ruler — to train us in the manhood. On the contrary. We have been dragged into the shabbiest occupations and we have been locked up in Ghettos where side by side we have degenerated. And when the gates were opened we were expected to have all the traits of a free people. If we had a united political leadership... we could proceed to the solution of the Jewish question.

The interview was broken off before Herzl was able to elaborate on the main points. On the next day he sent to Hirsch one of the greatest letters he, a master of letter writing, ever put down. It is filled with an unshakable certainty, the certainty of the way and the purpose. "This pen is a power," reads one of the first sentences, and in this vein others followed: "I am on my way" and "I hope you will live to see the radiant growth of my ideas.. You will then recall that Pentecost morning..." At the climax of this vehement exordium Herzl added the astonishing statement:

> Are you aware that you pursue a ghastly reactionary policy — worse than that of the most absolute autocracy? Fortunately your resources are insufficient. Your intentions are good, parbleu, je le sais bien. This is why I would like to give them direction. Do not permit yourself to hold it against me that I am fairly young. At my thirty-five years of age a man had become Minister of State in France, and Napoleon was Emperor.

Addressed to a man of sixty-five who, by his fabulous wealth and unparalleled philanthropic actions, had become a legendary benefactor in the whole world, the closing sentence was a challenge of extreme boldness. The sentence was far more a confession than a contention. The rest of the letter is devoted to a visionary and yet most precise outline of Herzl's future activity — an imperial activity as it might well be defined, not only by virtue of its object but because of the sovereign role which Herzl foresaw as his own in carrying out "the entire plan... everything directed from one center with purposive and foresighted vision." There followed an

almost hymnic praise of the flag! It reverberated unequivocally with the memories of those two Napoleonic scenes
which had become engraved in Herzl's soul. Thus, not an
abstract flag but the pierced flag before which Napoleon
had uncovered his head, which had set his soldiers in motion at Austerlitz and at the Berezina, dictated to Herzl
some of his most inspired lines:

> Finally, I would have had to tell you what flag I would
> unfurl and how. And then you would have asked in
> mockery, "A flag, what is that? A stick with a cloth
> rag?" No, a flag, sir, is more than that. With a flag
> you can lead men where you will — even into the Pro-
> mised Land. Men live and die for a flag, it is indeed
> the only thing for which they are willing to die in mas-
> ses, provided one educates them to it... Visions alone
> grip the souls of men. And whoever does not know
> how to deal in visions, may be an excellent, worthy,
> practical-minded person and even a benefactor in a
> big way, but he will never be a leader of men and no
> trace of him will remain... Out of this educated pro-
> letariat I will create the general staff and the cadres of
> the army which is to seek, discover and take over the
> Land...

When after the lapse of eight days no answer had arrived
from the Baron, Herzl began to suspect that his letter had
been a failure. "In my letter to Hirsch," reads an entry in
Herzl's Diary of June 11, 1895, "I wrote: 'In France, at my
35 years of age, men are Ministers of State, and Napoleon
was Emperor.' I now find that in my haste I stated my mean-

ing badly. As it stands, it smacks of megalomania. I merely meant that I too have a right to ponder political affairs and entertain the mature ideas of a statesman." Even if Herzl had not referred expressly to Napoleon, the Napoleonic spirit of the letter was manifest. A reader of the letter might have had sufficient reason for charging Herzl with megalomania. In fact, Herzl also entertained doubts on the subject as recorded in his diary on June 16:

> During these days I have been more than once afraid I was going mad. So wildly the streams of thought raced through my soul. A lifetime will not suffice to carry them out.
>
> But I am leaving behind me a spiritual legacy. To whom? To all men. I believe I shall be named among the great benefactors of mankind.
>
> Or is this belief the onset of megalomania?

And further on:

> I believe that for me life has ended and world history began... They will pray for me in the synagogues. But also in the churches.

On June 19 Herzl dispatched a long letter to Bismarck which he himself declared a turning point of his career. The letter was, like the first letter to Hirsch, a request for an interview. Thinking of Bismarck, Herzl could not suppress the thought of Napoleon. A diary entry of June 22 contained a short Plutarchian comparison:

> Who was greater: Napoleon or Bismarck? Napoleon. But his greatness was inharmonious. Napoleon was the sick superman, Bismarck the healthy one.

Herzl's unhesitating attribution of superiority to him whose
greatness was "inharmonious," was more than a detached
historical appreciation .Herzl was aware of the contradictions
of his own nature. From early youth he had been dissatisfied
with his work. Doubts and disillusionment sicknened his soul
and carried him to the edge of despair. The Jewish question
had, long before the definite solution, emerged from his
depths like a "rock of basalt" and tormented him bitterly.
These moods are reflected in an extraordinary letter to
Arthur Schnitzler written on June 23:

> Do you find me upset?... I am not, I was never in such
> happy high spirits. I do not think of dying, but of a life
> full of manly deeds that would effect all that was mean,
> vain and confused in my life and would reconcile every-
> body with me as I have reconciled myself through this
> work with everybody.

It was in this mood that Herzl reflected upon Napoleon, the
"sick superman" and once again acknowledged his greatness.

In a letter addressed (March 1, 1899) to the German
Kaiser he again referred to Napoleon:

> The idea to which I am devoted has in this century
> already touched a great monarch: Napoleon the First.
> The Paris Sanhedrin of the Jews of 1806 was, to be
> sure, a feeble reverberation of this idea. Was it that
> the thing has not matured yet at that time, that the
> Jews had not an efficient representative or were the
> poor means of communication the reason of that
> failure?

...The Jewish question has to be brought into the orbit of this sign: it can be solved in this manner. And what was impossible under the reign of Napoleon I is possible under that of Wilhelm II.

It was due to Herzl's historical insight that he clearly grasped the revivalist element in the Sanhedrin and that he ascribed to Napoleon the merit of having pursued the same goal he was aiming at. The passage describing the Sanhedrin seems to indicate that Herzl correctly supposed that a more substantial concept of a Jewish renaissance must have preceded the convocation of the Sanhedrin.

Another reference to Napoleon occurred in the Royal Palace Quirinal in Rome where Herzl was received in audience by the king Victor Emanuel (January 23, 1904). *"Il me mit à mon aise,"* Herzl recorded in his *Diaries,* "and in fact I chatted away a whole hour with him in the freest manner. He hasn't a trace of royalty's affectation. He has *son franc parler* and a lively mind. We were often both speaking at the same time carried away by the animation of our talk. It darted from one topic to another with such bewildering variety that now I find myself unable to reconstruct it." The pertinent entry in Herzl's *Diaries* records the main topics which were discussed: the equality enjoyed by the Jews in Italy; Palestine, which the king had visited on several occasions; Herzl's contact with the Grand Duke of Baden and Plehve; *Altneuland;* the Jordan and the Dead Sea Canal; Sabbatai Zevi and Jewish Messianism; the Jews in Eritrea, in China and elsewhere; the Sinai scheme and Uganda.

After the king expressed his opinion against Uganda, the conversation switched to Napoleon:

> When he [the king] spoke of the Sanhedrin summoned by Napoleon in 1806...
>
> "Napoleon had the idea of restoring the Jewish Nation, Sire."
>
> "No," argued the king, "he only wanted to use the Jews, who are scattered throughout the world, as his tools."
>
> "That, I found, was also Chamberlain's explanation."
>
> "It is fairly obvious," said the King.

Herzl unequivocally declared that Napoleon's intention was to restore the Jewish nation. There is a baffling definiteness in this historical observation. Moreover, Herzl's courteous reply to the king's differing opinion reveals that the question of Napoleon's attitude to the Jews had also been raised in his talk with Joseph Chamberlain, the British Colonial Secretary.

Although it was not given to Theodor Herzl to reap the fruits of his work, he laid the foundations upon which subsequent Zionist leaders were to build in later years. He thus has rightly been called the "Architect of the Balfour Declaration," and Napoleonic elements — whatever their amount might be — were through his medium involved in this structure. The effects which emanated from Napoleon's actions were, however, not confined to such an indirect influence. There is a historical link between Bonaparte's attack on Egypt and Syria and the operations which Great Britain in World War I undertook against Turkey. It was from Egypt

that Allenby started his 1917 expedition for the liberation
of Palestine. The campaign was a reverberation of the idea
which Bonaparte has injected into world politics. Bonaparte's
attempt to restore the Jewish people has also played an actual
part in the foundation of the Jewish National Home which
emerged from World War I — the first international recognition of Israel's claim to its restoration on the soil of the
Holy Land. Two of Herzl's leading followers, Israel Zangwill and Nahum Sokolow, continued his activity in this field.

Israel Zangwill was at the height of his literary reputation
when he became an ardent supporter of the Zionist cause
and thus added much to the political weight of Zionism.
In a lecture, *"The Ghetto,"* delivered at various places in
England in the late 'nineties, Zangwill surveyed the history
of the Diaspora, faced the question of Israel's future and
referred to Napoleon: "Napoleon, indeed, dreamed of reestablishing a Jewish kingdom in Palestine."[67]

In December, 1915, in an address to the Fabian Society,
he suggested that "if Britain took Palestine, she could make
no greater stroke of policy than to call in the Jews to regenerate it for her." But he pointed out, their mere immigration
would not be enough:

> It all requires a radically imaginative policy — a dealing
> in futures as well as in pasts by men ready to rescue
> human history from the monotonous factors of blood
> and gold. Napoleon, under the spell of the forty cen-
> turies that regarded him from the Pyramids, announced
> his design to restore the Jews to their land. Will Eng-
> land, with Egypt equally at her feet, carry out the plan

she foiled Napoleon in? Had she the power and genius
to do so, a new chapter would be opened in the history
of mankind, the ends of the ages would meet, and "the
tribe of the wandering foot and weary breast" which
for nineteen hundred years has prayed for Palestine
some twenty times a day would find itself to its holy
soil under the aegis of the greatest Empire in the world,
victorious after the greatest struggle in her history.[68]

In 1919 Nahum Sokolow published the first volume of his
monumental *History of Zionism*, with a preface by Lord
Balfour. This work, the result of admirable and original
research, was intended to offer the historical basis for the
recognition of the Jewish national claims to Palestine and
for the Balfour Declaration itself. Sokolow also dealt with
Bonaparte's Proclamation and with the Sanhedrin in three
chapters, recorded the report of the "Moniteur" and evalu-
ated Bonaparte's move. Sokolow's merit at having laid the
story of Napoleon's attempt to restore the Jewish people
as far as it was known at that time, on the table of the international gathering which was to decide upon the approval
of the Jewish National Home, can hardly be underestimated.
As the only historical precedent of the political measure then
under consideration, Napoleon's restorationist move was a
definite endorsement of the Balfour Declaration and thus
provided one of the strongest historical arguments for the
decision made by the Supreme Council of the Peace Conference at San Remo on April 24, 1920, to incorporate the
Balfour Declaration in the Treaty of Peace with Turkey.

Epilogue

In passing from the turbulent recent years, culminating in the catastrophe of European Jewry unparalleled in Jewish, indeed in entire human history and in the almost miraculous reemergence of the State of Israel, to the Napoleonic era, one cannot help being struck by the analogous and yet, at the same time, antithetic course of events. The encounter of the Jewish people with Napoleon was a turning point of Jewish history. For the first time, a modern statesman had envisaged the Jewish problem as a fundamental issue of international politics. His spectacular attempts at solution were based on the recognition of the Jewish national existence and aimed at the regeneration of the Jewish nation either by its restoration on the soil of the ancient homeland or by incorporating the newly organized nation into the vast empire he was about to create. In both schemes a personal political interest was involved. Moreover, the second experiment was neither free from an oppressive element nor from a tendency to achieve a radical assimilation of the Jewish people to the French and other surrounding nations. But the basic concept of preserving Jews and Judaism, above all, of linking the Jewry of the Emancipation era with the history of ancient Israel, permeated Bonaparte's restorationist move, as well as Napoleon's convocation of a representative all-Jewish body under the name of the Great Sanhedrin. Whether he fancied himself to be another Solomon who would rebuild the Temple of Jerusalem or a new Herod wielding authority over the dispersed nation, Napoleon considered the Jewish people as a partner in his world-wide plans.

The repercussions of the Proclamation and of Napoleon's
subsequent policy concerning the Jews justify the recognition
of these moves as one of the forces that finally brought about
the reestablishment of the State of Israel. They were, along-
side of the British movement for the Restoration of the Jews,
the main impulses coming from the non-Jewish world which
led towards the semi-Messianic goal of Israel. Bonaparte's
Proclamation and the convocation of the Great Sanhedrin
of Paris remained isolated phenomena in the century of
Emancipation; they lacked the powerful influence which the
uninterrupted flow of the British movement with its ever
growing literature and its outstanding champions — from
Joseph Priestley to Lord Shaftesbury and Colonel Charles
Henry Churchill, from Louis Way to George Eliot and Lau-
rence Oliphant — exerted on the minds of the British people
and on their statesmen. The dynamics of the British Empire,
one of the decisive driving forces toward the creation of the
Jewish National Home, surpass the impact of Napoleon's
historic move on behalf of the Jewish nation. Nevertheless,
Napoleon's restorationist attempts not only influenced the
founder of political Zionism and his followers, but also had
a lasting effect as a guarantee of the Messianic hope and a
silent endorsement of all the realistic plans for its fulfilment.
It was never forgotten by those who dreamed of Israel's revival that on the threshold of the nineteenth century, the
dream almost came true.

As a miraculous climax of the historical connections between Bonaparte's attempt to restore the Jewish nation and
the reestablishment of the State of Israel the text of the Proclamation to the "rightful heirs of Palestine" came to light

amidst the most crucial crisis of the Jewish people and thus could bear witness to the political claims of the Jews to the Land of Israel. The symbolic significance of this testimony was poignantly stressed by the simultaneous emergence of Rabbi Aaron's letter to the Children of Israel. For even when, after a period of agonizing trials, the Resolution of the General Assembly of the United Nations sanctioned the establishment of the Jewish State the Jewish people had still to learn another lesson clearly taught by the Napoleonic documents. In fact, 150 years after the "warranty of the French nation" promised by Bonaparte's call, the pledges of many nations would hardly have proved effective, if the Jews of the Land of Israel had not taken unto themselves "the wings of the eagle and the strength of the lioness."

NOTES

1 *The New Judea*, XVI (1940), pp. 189 f.; XVII (1941), pp. 18 f., 36—38.
2 "Napoleon be-Erez Israel" (Hebrew) in: *Sefer ha-Yovel le-Professor Dinaburg* (1949), pp. 262—288.
3 C. Roth, *The History of the Jews of Italy* (1946), p. 83.
4 N. Tomich, *Napoléon Ecrivain* (1952), p. 297.
5 Las Casas, *Mémoires* (1823), I, p. 78.
6 E. Jones, *Sigmund Freud*, III (1957), p. 422 f.
7 F. Masson, *Napoléon Inconnu* (1895) I, p. 318.
8 *ibid.*, p. 466; see also, pp. 260, 318.
9 *ibid.*, p. 48.
10 *ibid.*, p. 273.
11 Napoleon's letters, notes, memoranda, proclamation, etc. are chronologically arranged in his complete *Correspondences*.
12 C. Roth, *Italy*, pp. 425 ff.; see also A. Milano, *Storia degli ebrei in Italia* (1963), pp. 343 ff.
13 F. Charles-Roux, *Les Origines de l'Expédition d'Egypte* (1910).
14 F. Kobler, *The Vision Was There* (1956).
   B. W. Tuchman, *Bible & Sword* (1956).
   N. M. Gelber, *Zur Vorgeschichte des Zionismus* (1927).
   On Pre-Zionism in America see I. S. Meyer (ed.), *Early History of Zionism in America* & M. Davis (ed.), *Israel, Its Role in Civilization* (1956).
   In Hebrew: M. Verete, "The Idea of the Restoration of Israel in Protestant Thought in England in the years 1790—1840," in *Zion*, XXXII (1968), pp. 145—179.
15 C. Roth, *Anglo-Jewish Letters* (1938), pp. 201 ff.
16 R. Matthews, *English Messiahs* (1936).

[17] H.-J. Schoeps, *Barockjuden, Christen Judenchristen* (1965);
G. H. Dodge, *The Political Theory of the Huguenots of the Dispersion* (1951);
N. M. Gelber, *Vorgeschichte.*

[18] M. Oulie, *Le Prince de Ligne* (1926), pp. 142 ff., 174 ff.

[19] C. Roth, "The Jews of Malta," in: *Transactions of the Jewish Historical Society of England,* XII (1931), pp. 187—251.

[20] The author's narrative is based primarily upon
J. C. Herold, *Bonaparte in Egypt* (1963);
P. G. Elgood, *Bonaparte's Adventure in Egypt* (1936).

[21] A. Alcais, *Napoléon et la Religion* (1923), p. 44.

[22] Napoleon, *Campagnes d'Egypte et de Syrie.*

[23] Bourienne, *Mémoire de M. de Bourienne sur Napoléon,* p. 217.

[24] Elgood, *Bonaparte's Adventure in Egypt,* p. 205.

[25] Y. Rivkind, "Dapim Bodedim" (Hebrew in: *Jerushalayim,* dedicated to A. M. Luncz [1928]), p. 143.

[26] Bourrienne, p. 243.

[27] Napoleon, *Campagnes.*

[28] *ibid.*

[29] R. B. Holtman, *Napoleonic Propaganda* (1950), pp. 187 ff.

[30] S. W. Baron, *A Social & Religious History of the Jews,* II (1937), p. 327.

[31] B. W. Tuchman, p. 105.

[32] Las Casas, p. 247.

[33] Guedalla, p. 28 f.

[34] B. Holtmann.

[35] A. S. Yahuda, "Conception d'un état juif par Napoléon," in *Evidences* (1951), no. 19, May—June, pp. 5—7;
also in: *Zion* (incorporating *The New Judea)* I (1950), No. 7, pp. 29—34.

[36] R. Southey, III, 170.

[37] G. Scholem, *Major Trends in Jewish Mysticism* (1946).

[38] V. Zacek, "Zwei Beiträge zur Geschichte des Frankismus in den bohemischen Ländern," in *Jahrbuch der Czechoslovakischen Republik,* 9 (1938), pp. 348—410.

[39] H. Graetz, *History of the Jews, V* (1949), p. 400.

40 S. Dubnow, *Weltgeschichte des jüdischen Volkes*, XIV (1928), p. 134.

41 Gelber, *Vorgeschichte*, p. 280.

42 B. Z. Dinaburg, *Mevassre la-Zionut* (1938).

43 M. Liber, "Les Juifs et la Convocation des Etats Généraux," in: *Revue des Etudes Juives* (serialized), LXIII—LXVI (1912—1913) and *idem*, "Napoléon & les Juifs," *ibid.* (serialized) LXXI—LXXII (1920—1921), p. 143.

44 Lemoine, *Napoléon et les Juifs* (1900), p. 53 f.

45 M. Liber, *Napoléon*, passim.

46 E. D. Pasquier, *Mémoires*, p. 297.

47 *ibid.*, p. 295.

48 R. Anchel, pp. 187—189.

49 D. Tama, *Transactions*, pp. 270—273.

50 Colber, *Napoleon*, p. 283.

51 *idem.*, "La police autrichienne et la Sanhedrin," in *Revue des Etudes Juives*, LXXXII (1927), pp. 141—143.

52 Lemoine, p. 223.

53 J. A. C. Chaptal, *Mes Souvenirs sur Napoléon* (1893), pp. 242 f.

54 Anchel, p. 220.

55 Colber, *Napoleon*, p. 282.

56 *idem, ibid.*, pp. 283 f.

57 S. Z. Pipes, "Napoleon in Folklore," in: *Yivo Annal of Jewish Social Sciences*, I (1946), pp. 294—304.

58 T. Ussher, *Napoleon's Last Voyage* (1966), p. 102.

59 *American Jewish Historical Society Proceedings*, XXVII (1920), pp. 140—141.
See also: J. J. Shulim, "Napoleon as the Jewish Messiah: Some Contemporary Conceptions in Vienna," in: *Jewish Social Studies*, VII (1945), pp. 275—280.

60 O'Meara, I, pp. 113—114.

61 For a full treatment, see: P. Holzhansen, *Heine und Napoleon* (1903), and the *Heine Bibliographie*, G. Wilhelm (ed.) II (1960), p. 131 no. 2213—2226 and p. 181 no. 3042-3-51.

62 J.-R. Bloch, Napoleon & ...

63 J. Parkes, "Lewis Way & his Times," in: *Transactions JHSE*, XX (1959—1961), pp. 189—202; and Gelber, *Vorgeschichte*, pp. 62 ff.

64 I. Goldberg, *Major Noah* (1936); see index & bibliography.

65 F. Kobler, "Charles Henry Churchill," in *Herzl Yearbook*, IV (1961), pp. 1—67; I. Bentwich & J. M. Shaftesley, "Forerunners of Zionism in the Victorian Era," in: J. M. Shaftesley (ed.), *Remember the Days* (1966), pp. 207—244.

66 H. Zohn (ed.) *The Complete Diaries of T. Herzl* (1960);
M. Lowenthal (ed.), *The Diaries of Theodor Herzl* (1958);
A. Bein, *Theodor Herzl* (1964).

67 I. Zangwill, *Speeches.*

68 *idem, The Voice of Jerusalem.*